The Prayer of Agreement:
Repositioning Ourselves with God

Dr. Estelle E. Gross

Copyright © 2008 by Dr. Estelle E. Gross

The Prayer of Agreement:
Repositioning Ourselves with God
by Dr. Estelle E. Gross

Printed in the United States of America

ISBN 978-1-60647-478-5

All rights reserved solely by the author. The author guarantees all contents are original and do not infringe upon the legal rights of any other person or work. No part of this publication may be reproduced, stored in a retrieval system or transmitted in any form or by any means— for example, electronic, photocopy, recording—without the prior written permission of the author. The only exception is brief quotations in printed reviews. The views expressed in this book are not necessarily those of the publisher.

Unless otherwise indicated, all Scripture quotations are taken from the *Holy Bible*, New International Version ®, copyright © 1973, 1978, 1984 by International Bible Society. Used by permission of Zondervan Publishing House. All rights reserved.

Scriptures marked NKJV are taken from the *Holy Bible*, New King James Version. Copyright ©1982, 1994 by Thomas Nelson Publishers. Used by permission. All rights reserved.

Library of Congress Cataloging-in-Publication Data

Gross, Estelle.

The Prayer of Agreement
The Prayer of Agreement: what the twenty-first century church understands about the prayer of agreement can reposition it as a vehicle to extend God's will on earth as it is in heaven.

www.xulonpress.com

TOUCHING HEAVEN IN PRAYER

THE PROMISES

*"I tell you the truth, whatever you bind on earth
will be bound in heaven,
and whatever you loose on earth will be loosed in heaven.
Again, I tell you
that if two of you agree on earth about anything you ask for,
it will be done for you by My Father in heaven.
For where two or three come together in My name,
there am I with them."*
Matthew 18:18-20

CONTENTS

Introduction		xi
Chapter One:	Exploring the Promises	13
Section One:	**Agreements**	**23**
Chapter Two:	The Dynamics of Agreement	23
Chapter Three:	Agreements of the Godhead	33
Chapter Four:	Agreements with Mankind	41
Section Two:	**Choices**	**53**
Chapter Five:	The Choice that Caused Loss	53
Chapter Six:	The Unforeseen Consequences	59
Chapter Seven:	The Choice that Restores	67
Section Three:	**Struggles**	**77**
Chapter Eight:	The Incessant Struggles	77
Chapter Nine:	Engaging the Enemy: Understanding His Tactics	87
Chapter Ten:	Engaging the Enemy: Know How to Resist	95
Section Four:	**Repositioning**	**103**
Chapter Eleven:	Repositioning Ourselves with God	103
Section Five:	**Prayer**	**109**
Chapter Twelve:	The Heart of God	109
Chapter Thirteen:	The Heart of God's Intercessor	117

FORWARD

There is nothing more important to the twenty-first century church today than a proper understanding of God's promises to us, particularly as related to prayer. Dr. Estelle Gross, a member of my church, is not only a person of keen insight into God's promises, but also a person gifted in communicating those Biblical principles to receptive believers. The book is written so that both clergy and laity can understand it. Of particular benefit are the principles of praying in agreement, the role of the pray-er, and the influence prayer can have in both the seen and unseen in our daily life. More importantly, she reminds each of us, "…The prayer of agreement gives God an open door to intervene in the affairs of mankind."

My prayer is that those who read these pages will "hear" and embrace Dr. Gross' joy, which permeates the entire book. This book truly reflects the values of her life that are on display for His sake.

Dr. Gross, please receive my appreciation for the Biblical integrity of your text, the enthusiasm reflected in its' content, and the Kingdom contribution represented by its' publication.

Dr. Phillip Bolerjack
Senior/Lead Pastor
Marley Park Church of the Nazarene
Glen Burnie, Maryland, USA

INTRODUCTION

God desires a relationship with all mankind and us. A relationship of purpose and significance awaits us. Repositioning ourselves with God is a choice, one that will allow us the privilege to extend God's kingdom on earth. God has given us so many rich and precious promises that are obtainable only as we draw near to Him. Exploring the promises connected with the prayer of agreement has taken me from Genesis to Revelation. No other passage of Scripture has sent my mind racing, as has this Matthew 18:18-20 passage, which reveals the unlimited impact of the prayers of agreement.

I trust you will join the search with me as we discover how the principles of God's promises work: why Jesus gave us, His disciples, such powerful promises; why agreement is so vital to the promises being fulfilled; and the purpose for which these promises have been given to us.

Meditation on this passage reveals some important truths that can bring us back into unity with God, help restore what was lost in the Garden of Eden, and once again join earth and heaven. Praying God's *"kingdom to come and (His) will (to) be done on earth as it is in heaven"* will take on new meaning.

As we study the Word, we learn of God's great love for all mankind: the unsaved, the immature believer, and the growing Christian. God knew what it would cost Him when He gave us freewill. Freewill allows each individual to make decisions either to accept God's will or reject it. Such was the case with Adam and his wife, Eve, when they chose to reject God's Word, which broke their fellowship with their Creator. Few have come to realize that to reject God's word is to reject God. To reject God is to reject His Kingdom.

This act of disobedience set many unforeseen consequences into motion. There was a shift of power, man lost his dominion over earth, an unseen enemy moved into position, and communication between heaven and earth was broken. Consequently, the will of God was hindered from taking place on earth. This set into motion the ingredients for earthly kingdoms. These earthly kingdoms of darkness can be changed only as we understand our role and participate in the salvation of souls by prayer and presenting the gospel. Nations are changed as the people who make up the nations are changed—translated from the kingdom of darkness to the kingdom of light.

With broken communications and the loss of dominion, many troubles and crises have resulted in our world. God's desire to communicate with all mankind has not changed. The communion between God and man is restored today when we accept Christ Jesus as our Savior, accept our responsibility to co-labor with Him through prayer, and accept our responsibility to advance the kingdom of God.

In our daily walk we must understand the tactics of the unseen enemy that successfully undermined God's plan for mankind in the Garden. It will help us to know the personal commitment needed to live in communication with God, exercise the authority returned to us in Christ Jesus, and offer prayers that connect heaven and earth once again.

Our focus needs to be on the truth that God's kingdom can come to earth and that it is possible for His will to be manifested here as it is in heaven when we make ourselves available to pray with others. Are you ready?

CHAPTER ONE

EXPLORING THE PROMISES

*"Let me understand the teaching of your precepts;
then I will meditate on your wonders."*
Psalms 119:27

EXPLORING THE PROMISES

"I tell you the truth, whatever you bind on earth will be bound in heaven, and whatever you loose on earth will be loosed in heaven. Again I tell you that if two of you on earth agree about anything you ask for, it will be done for you by My Father in heaven. For where two or three come together in My name, there am I with them." Matthew 18:18-20

There are three promises available to us in this passage that alert us to our responsibility to both pray and act in accordance with the will and purposes of God. Man lost his dominion over earth in the Fall. Jesus knew He would restore dominion of earth back to mankind. These promises provide insight in how to exercise the restored dominion and once again participate in extending God's kingdom on earth.

1. Our prayers and actions on earth can influence what happens in the heavenly realm.

2. Our prayer of agreement on earth brings about answers from our Father in heaven.

3. Our use of Jesus' name brings results.

Together let us explore these tremendous promises that Jesus is giving us, His disciples. Has Jesus handed us a blank check? I think it is more like a promissory note that requires the proper identification to cash. We must use biblical principles and present the proper identification to collect on these promises. *"For no matter how many promises God has made they are yes in Christ..."* 2 Corinthians 1:20.

In light of the broken communications caused by sin, God has given believers an opportunity to co-labor with Him once again. Adam, in communication with God, extended the kingdom of God on earth. There was no need of promises, just obedience. The sacrifice of Jesus Christ, the Lamb of God, fulfilled the promise given Adam before he was expelled from the Garden.

Jesus defeated Adam's unseen enemy on the Cross. Receiving Jesus Christ as our Savior restores us to the role of ambassadors. As diplomatic officials, our actions are to represent and extend the kingdom of God on earth. Whatever we pray should have as its core purpose to advance the kingdom of God and give Him glory. Our heavenly Father awaits our prayers to intervene in the affairs of men.

Jesus provides instructions that reveal the purpose and results of effective praying. *"If you remain in me and my words remain in you, ask whatever you wish, and it will be given you. This is to my Father's glory, that you bear much fruit showing yourself to be my disciples"* John 15:7-8. The instructions are to remain in Jesus, who provides our identity; and remain in the Word, which provides the boundaries for "whatever" we ask.

There appears to be a three-fold purpose: (1) prayers bear fruit, (2) fruit gives glory to the Father, and (3) the results reveal that the fruit-bearers are disciples of Jesus. Since Jesus came to seek and save the lost, our fruit is the winning of the lost back to God. Prayers open the door for God's will to be manifested on earth, an excellent reason why there is response from the Father when we pray in agreement.

The ability to influence heaven by our actions on earth is an awesome possibility. God's promises should be the basis for our motivation. Abraham believed the Lord, and God credited it to him for righteousness (Genesis 15:6). Abraham obeyed God and qualified for the promise. Through his promised seed we have a Savior, Jesus Christ. What will we offer to our world as we believers act on these three promises?

Our commitment to bring the Father glory should be kept in focus. Our study uncovers the mysteries connected with the prayer of agreement. Mysteries such as prayer influence the heavenly realm and brings a response from the Father.

INFLUENCES THE HEAVENLY REALM

Connecting Heaven and Earth

"Whatever you bind on earth will be bound in heaven, and whatever you loose on earth will be loosed in heaven." What a personal promise! Jesus appears to be speaking to each of us directly. Unlimited impact: Our prayers and actions on earth have an effect on things in heaven. This mystery is understood when we learn that our struggles are not against flesh and blood, but against rulers, authorities, and spiritual forces of evil in the heavenly realm. We need to influence that which influences our world. It can be done only through prayer. A few examples of our influence are seen in Chapter 2: "The Dynamics of Agreement."

Involving the Seen and Unseen

Man was given dominion over the earth: seen and unseen. No, man knew nothing about the unseen—not unlike many individuals in our day. *"The weapons of our warfare are not carnal, but mighty through God to the pulling down of the strongholds"* 2 Corinthians 10:4 (KJV). We will learn of the tools the enemy uses to develop strongholds in our lives in Chapter 7, "The Incessant Struggles." Prayer is our weapon when we use the Word.

Man lost his dominion in his act of disobedience but through Jesus Christ dominion has been returned to mankind. However, only believers in Christ Jesus can once again exercise the authority given to them in the Garden. The key now is for believers to learn how to make use of the returned dominion. The unseen, however, still has influence in our world because of unbelievers and immature believers. Satan has dominion over unbelievers because they are still serving him. Jesus said to the Jews, *"You belong to your father, the devil, and you want to carry out your father's desire"* John 8:44a. The immature believer has not yet learned how to discern the tactics of the enemy. Those falling under Satan's influence hinder the plans of God from being manifested on earth.

With the promise of the Father answering our prayers of agreement, the unseen can be bound and the seen loosed from the control of Satan. Examples of how the seen and unseen are affected thru prayer are discussed in Chapter 2, "The Dynamics of Agreement."

BRINGS THE FATHER'S RESPONSE

Jesus states that if two agree on earth about anything they ask, His Father in heaven will do it. The Greek word for "agree" literally means, "to sound together," and can be translated "to be in accord" as musical instruments are tuned together. Our relationship with Jesus enables us to call God our Father. *"Because you are sons, God sent the Spirit of his Son into our hearts, the Spirit who calls out "Abba Father'"* Galatians 4:6.

There is another promise that comes with agreement. Psalm 133 states, *"Behold how good and how pleasant it is for brethren to dwell together in unity... for there the Lord commanded the blessing..."* (NKJV). Let us double the results by coming in unity to pray. A commanded blessing from God is worth going after!

We have the assurance of the Father's involvement when we come together to pray in agreement about "Whatever." As we abide in the Word, we discover that our "whatever" is connected with establishing God's kingdom on earth. We learn to look at the various situations and pray for God's kingdom to come. Our prayers go up in unison as the sound of musical instruments in harmony. This means that we should spend some time together discussing our needs and concerns, and presenting them to our Father in heaven. This is reason enough for us to develop good relationships with our prayer partner(s) and together take our concerns and those that touch the heart of God to our Father in prayer.

THE NAME OF JESUS BRINGS RESULTS

Prayer offered in Jesus' name assures His presence

Jesus stated that when two or three individuals gather in His name, He would be present. When was the last time you took advantage of this promise? Talking about restoring relationships with the Father—this is the way to go!

This promise of God's presence was given to the Israelites and they declared: *"What other nation is so great as to have their gods near them the way the Lord our God is near us whenever we pray to him"* Deuteronomy 4:7. This name was not to be used in vain. The Israelites were told, *"You shall not take the name of the Lord your God in vain, for the Lord will not hold him guiltless who takes His name in vain"* Exodus 20:7 (NKJV). It may be helpful to know that the Father, Son, and the Holy Spirit share the same name. It reveals to us why Jesus told the disciples in the Lord's Prayer to hallow (make holy) the Father's name. It is the name of the Godhead.

Father and Son: *"I am come in my Father's name"* John 5:43 (KJV).

Son: *"Call his name Jesus"* Luke 1:3, which means Jehovah is salvation.

Spirit: *"But the Comforter, which is the Holy Spirit, whom the Father will send in my name..."* John 14:26a (KJV).

The disciples were told to baptize believers in all nations in the name of the Father and of the Son and of the Holy Spirit (Matthew 28:19). Peter understood that the name of Jesus encompassed the Father, Son, and the Holy Spirit. On the day of Pentecost, Peter told the devout men, *"Repent and be baptized every one of you, in the name of Jesus Christ for the forgiveness of sins"* Acts 2:38. Paul understood also and told the disciples in Ephesus to be baptized in the name of Jesus. *"When they heard this, they were baptized in the name of the Lord Jesus"* Acts 19:3. Every believer who obeys this mandate hallows the name of the Father when they are baptized in the name of Jesus.

Prayer in Jesus' name provides our authority

Jesus told His disciples *"All authority in heaven and earth has been given to me. Therefore go and make disciples of all nations, baptizing them in the name of the Father and of the Son and of the Holy Spirit"* Matthew 28:18-19. In that all encompassing authority, we are told to make disciples of all nations. We use this delegated authority in prayer when we gather in His name, which empowers us to go into the world and accomplish His mission of making disciples.

Coming together to pray in His name helps us restore the union and communication lost in the Garden of Eden. The whole Godhead is called when we use the name of Jesus. This restored relationship means we do not have to wait for God to visit us, we can come into His presence by gathering in His name. God's kingdom is then established on earth as man and God are united in Jesus.

Prayer offered in Jesus' name assures answers

Jesus told his disciples, "*And I will do whatever you ask in my name, so that the Son may bring glory to the Father. You may ask me for anything in my name, and I will do it*" John 14:13-14.

As we understand the promises tied into these three verses, they reveal that we must be involved in our world. Our actions on earth influence what goes on in the heavens. Coming together in agreement in prayer brings a commanded blessing. Jesus states that our heavenly Father will respond and do whatever we ask. In addition, Jesus has instructed us to gather in His name with the promise of His presence. Our first agreement is with God. When we believe His Word, we will act on it. Our second agreement is with our prayer partner(s) in coming together and praying in His name. The Bible is filled with promises that our prayers will get results.

The agreement between God and man was broken in the Garden of Eden. Two people, Adam and Eve, agreed to disobey God. Now we have an opportunity to find another person who will agree to obey God with marvelous results. Prayer in the name of Jesus can open heaven's door for restored relationship with God. A look at the agreements of the Godhead and agreements with mankind in Chapters 3 and 4 will assure us that God's plan for mankind is still available to us. Can we believe God, "*For all the promises of God in Him are Yes, and in Him Amen, to the glory of God through us*" 2 Corinthians 1:20? When the Word is mixed with faith, it is profitable!

SECTION ONE: AGREEMENTS

CHAPTER TWO

THE DYNAMICS OF AGREEMENT

"Call to me and I will answer you and tell you great and unsearchable things you do not know."
Jeremiah 33:3

THE DYNAMICS OF AGREEMENT

"Again, I tell you that if two of you on earth agree about anything you ask for, it will be done for you by my Father in heaven." Matthew 18:19

The prayer of agreement gives God an open door to intervene in the affairs of mankind. *"The highest heavens belong to the Lord, but the earth He has given to man"* Psalms 115:16. God is in the highest heavens; Satan and his fallen angels operate in the heavenly realms and cause man's struggles on earth. Man lost dominion over the earth. This dominion was handed over to Satan at the fall and restored to mankind by the finish work of Jesus Christ on the cross.

Because of the fallen state of mankind and the continued activities of Satan, mankind is involved in various types of warfare: among nations, between individuals, with unseen spiritual beings, and within ourselves. Paul states it this way, *"...I see another law at work in the members of my body, waging war against the law of my mind and making me a prisoner of the law of sin at work within my members"* Romans 7:23. These circumstances do not bring the desired results.

Working on our own, we are left warring against one another, battling against the unseen forces of darkness, and grabbing for ideas that only intensify the problems. It is usually in these defeating situations that we realize our need for godly intervention. The dominion of earth has been handed back over to mankind. However, only believers in prayer—those who understand the principles and purposes of God—experience the dynamic results of the power of agreement.

How the principles work

The first promise of a Savior was given to Adam and Eve after the Fall. God told the serpent that He would put enmity between him and the woman. Abraham received God's promise that all families of the earth would be blessed through Him. That promise spoke of the Savior. And it is here that we learn that the enmity would be with a person. The promise given David informed us that the Savior would be King. In each case it took at least one individual to believe God and respond in obedience to His promise.

To believe and respond in obedience means we must first know the promises of God before we can pray and return them to God. The only way to know the promises is to know the Word of God. When David received the Word that God would establish his name, his house, and his kingdom, he went in and sat before God and literally claimed the promise in prayer (2 Samuel 7):

"Then King David went in and sat before the Lord and he said, 'Who am I, O Sovereign Lord, and what is my family, that you have brought me this far? And as if this were not enough in your sight, O Sovereign Lord, you have also spoken about the future of the house of your servant. Is this your usual way of dealing with man, O Sovereign Lord?...For the sake of your word and according to your will, you have done this great thing and made it known to your servant... And now, Lord God, keep forever the promise

you have made concerning your servant and his house. Do as you promised, so that your name will be great forever..." 2 Samuel 7:18-26a.

First, David learns of the promise; second he believes the promise and declares that God's Words are trustworthy (vs. 28); third, he requests that God fulfill His promise; and fourth, he knew the purpose of the promise: that God's name would be made great forever and men will know the Lord Almighty is God. It is just that simple.

God has proven His love for mankind from creation. Having received Jesus Christ as Savior, we have experienced God's answered promise to Adam, Abraham, and David. Jesus reveals to us how to respond to the promises of God so we, too, can stand in the position of Abraham and David through the impact of prayer. Embracing the promises by following the instructions will reposition us to reclaim our dominion lost in the Fall.

Jesus said, *"If you remain in me, and my words remain in you, ask whatever you wish, and it will be given you. This is to my Father's glory, that you bear much fruit, showing yourselves to be my disciples"* John 15:7-8. Principles: Believe God, Remain in Jesus, Remain in the Word, Ask what you wish, and Keep in focus that answered prayers bring the Father glory. Will you put God's principles into operation?

Why Jesus gave us the promise

By His death and resurrection, Jesus Christ restored dominion of earth to mankind. Learning how to operate in our delegated authority to properly exercise dominion on earth takes a lifetime. As we operate in the authority, we begin to restore what was lost in the Fall—the establishment of God's kingdom on earth.

As we gather in the prayer of agreement with the Word of God as our guide and in the authority we receive from

Jesus, we can ask whatever we will. In prayer, God is able to move on our behalf giving results that reveal the glory of the Father.

God's will and purposes are re-established in our communication with God. As we obey, God's will is accomplished and His purposes are manifested on earth as it is in heaven. Mankind will come to know that the Lord Almighty is God. This is how His kingdom is established on earth. You and I have the opportunity to exercise our authority on earth as we pray the will of God resulting in the Son revealing the Father's glory on earth.

Why agreement is necessary

God has promised to honor the requests of believers committed to pray together, so this is reason enough to do it. God's Word is life and spirit, and reveals what God wants to accomplish. The way we accept those promises is to pray God's Word. The Word will bring life to the situation in which we live. Agreement in obedience to the promises will permit the glory of God on earth to be revealed. As individuals and the church move into agreement with God, the kingdoms of this world will lose their powers. The power of agreement is seen in Genesis, Chapter 11. After the flood God directed Noah and his sons to be fruitful, increase in number, and fill the earth. Instead they decided to build a city, and a tower, whose top would reach unto heaven. They wanted to make a name for themselves instead of scattering abroad and filling the earth. Their actions caught the attention of the Godhead. *"The Lord said, if as one people speaking the same language, they have begun to do this, then nothing they plan to do will be impossible for them"* Genesis 11:6.

Agreement, even in disobedience, is powerful. Just imagine: nothing they planned to do would be impossible for them. God stopped the unity—the agreement of these people to disobey Him. The Godhead agreed to go down and confound their language so they would not be able to understand one another. The place was called Babel. God scattered them across the face of all the earth. This powerful act of disobedience led to the establishment of the kingdoms of this world.

How much more could be accomplished when we agree to pray God's will in obedience to His Word. Our world is now filled with many kingdoms. Until we make ourselves available to God we will not see God's kingdom extended to earth. God has given us a powerful tool—agreement.

Prayer Connects Heaven and Earth

We have an example in Scripture of a group of believers that had no earthly solution for their problem. Operating on God's promises, this group of believers gathered to pray, and opened the portal between heaven and earth.

In Acts, Chapter 12, the church was being persecuted. King Herod had killed James, the brother of John, with the sword. When Herod saw that it pleased the Jews, he proceeded to seize Peter and intended to bring him out for public trial. The church was intentional in their prayers for Peter.

They agreed that they were helpless to get Peter out of jail, that Peter's life was in danger, and that something needed to be done. While these believers gathered in agreement on earth, the Father in heaven dispatched an angel to earth to release Peter from the grips of Herod.

The angel instructed Peter to put on his garment and follow him. Together they walked past the first and second guard post unseen; the gate of the city opened without help. The band of believers were unaware of all the activities taking place because they agreed to gather in prayer requesting God's help.

The Prayer of Agreement Brings Results

We can be sure that Satan was behind the political reasons for Herod's desire to destroy Peter; Satan was out to stop the growth of the church. Through prayer, the enemy was bound in the heavenly realm, Herod and the Jews were bound on earth, and the Father's response brought praise and thanks from these believers. Peter was delivered.

God's desire to communicate with mankind has not changed. He is waiting for us to present Him the opportunity to apply His solution to our earthly dilemmas. When His answers are manifested, God's glory is revealed and believers have properly used their delegated authority.

Battling on Two Fronts: Physical and Spiritual

The dynamics involved in agreement are seen clearly in Exodus, Chapter 17. Here Moses and Joshua included prayer in their conflict. They planned to fight the battle on two fronts: the seen (physical) and the unseen (spiritual)

Their prayer of agreement allowed their actions on earth to mysteriously affect things in heaven. Remember, Jesus tells us that our Father in heaven will do what we ask for on earth. The need for this action is seen as Moses and Joshua agree to fight the Amalekites at Rephidim on both the physical and spiritual plain.

The Amalekites attacked the Israelites. No reason is given for the attack. The Israelites had been quarreling because there was no water in Rephidim. Was it this quarreling spirit that opened the door for the enemy? Moses, the leader of his people, directed Joshua to select men to go out to fight the physical battle, while he would take men to the top of the hill to fight the spiritual battle.

As long as Moses' hands were lifted to God, the Israelites were winning the battle. When Moses' hands were down, the

Amalekites were winning. Prayer made all the difference in this battle.

There was unity of purpose in this passage. Moses and Joshua agreed to fight the enemy. Joshua was able to get men to agree with him to go into battle to fight the enemy, which was seen. Moses was able to get Aaron and Hur to agree to go up the mountain with him to pray. They were fighting against an unseen force that seemed somehow to empower the seen, the Amalekites.

Coming into agreement does not mean we will *say* and *do* the same thing, but that we will *agree to accomplish the same thing*: God's purpose. This could be doing different tasks to bring about the same purpose.

Prayer of Agreement Brings the Father's Response

How can you logically explain why Moses' raised hands made a difference in the warfare? Why did his hands influence Joshua on the battlefield? Before Abraham defeated Chedorlaomer and the kings allied with him, He had raised his hand to the Lord God Most High (Genesis 15:17-24). With 318 men trained in his household, Abraham defeated five kings. God has been responding to requests for His help and He has responded by giving them victory.

We will discuss our incessant struggles with rulers, authorities, the power of this dark world, and against the spiritual forces of evil in the heavenly realms in Section 3, "Struggles." This Exodus passage reveals that unseen forces are at work in our warfare. The actions of Joshua and Moses reveal the faithfulness of God to respond to His children. What area of concern do you have for your family, church, or world? Your concerns could be burdens given to you by God to call you into partnership with Him by means of prayer. Once we accept that we have unseen enemies, the next step is to learn how to engage the enemy using the prayer of agreement given us in this Matthew passage.

In order to understand the dynamics of agreement, it might help us to review the agreements of the Godhead and the agreements of the Godhead with mankind. The Bible opens with the agreements of the Godhead working in unison in the creation of heaven and earth, in the creation of mankind, and in the plan for the redemption of mankind.

These agreements reveal God's love and purpose for mankind. Agreeing with God will motivate us to identify our prayer partner. Together we can work in unison with God and one another to fulfill God's purpose and see His kingdom established on earth as it is in heaven. May we begin to understand the significance of our decisions to pray or not to pray, the struggles involved in spiritual warfare, and how we can reposition ourselves with God. Exploring these promises will take us into the heart of God and that of His intercessor.

Let the journey begin.

CHAPTER THREE

AGREEMENTS OF THE GODHEAD

*"The Lord Almighty has sworn,
Surely, as I have planned, so it will be,
and as I have purposed, so it will stand."*
Isaiah 14:24

AGREEMENTS OF THE GODHEAD

Agreement in Creation

"In the beginning God created the heavens and the earth. Now the earth was formless and empty, darkness was over the surface of the deep, and the Spirit of God was hovering over the waters. And God said, "Let there be light and there was light" Genesis 1:1-3.

Scripture states that Elohim (plural for God) created the heavens and the earth. This reveals the power of unity demonstrated by the Godhead. We see the Holy Spirit at work hovering over the face of the water, and the Word manifesting what God spoke. From this act we see that agreement is more than doing the same thing. God, the Spirit, and the Word each had their own roles in creation—and with powerful results. Each had different tasks with the same purpose.

Our world was brought into existence by the unity of the Godhead, and it would make sense that God would bless our efforts when we work in unity with one another and with Him. It is interesting that the first words Elohim spoke was *"Let there be light, and there was light."* The world was not to be left in darkness. We learn that God's word brings light.

Agreement in the Creation of Man

"Then God said, Let us make man in our image, in our likeness, and let them rule over the fish of the sea and the birds of the air, the livestock, over all the earth, and over all the creatures that move along the ground" Genesis **1:26**.

Elohim created man with purpose. God said, *"Let us make man."* And in the same sentence said *"let them rule."* The dominion of man was to be over *"all the earth, and over all the creatures that move along the ground."* This is what God intended. It was not for man to be in submission to the plants of the earth as so many are today with drugs. Man had dominion over all the earth and was in communion with God. The kingdom of God reigned on earth as God and man were in fellowship in the Garden of Eden.

Everything was in the Garden that would ensure man could obtain eternal life and exercise freewill. God wanted man to love and obey Him freely, so even in the Garden there was opportunity for man to obey or disobey Him. In the midst of the Garden stood the tree of life and the tree of the knowledge of good and evil, which man was not to eat if he wanted to live. Man's choice to obey God was manifested as long as the forbidden tree stood untouched. God's kingdom extended to earth in man's obedience.

God knew what it would cost Him to give man freewill. Yet, He loved man so much that He made plans for his restoration should disobedience take place. This was a thought-out decision. The Godhead agreed to make man in His image and likeness and to give him dominion over all the earth. This means the Godhead was in harmony with this action. There was oneness of purpose.

Jesus tells His disciples that if two of them would be in harmony or in oneness of purpose in anything they ask on earth, the Father in heaven would do it. Seeing what oneness of the Godhead accomplished in Creation, it should help us understand what the power of oneness can accomplish in prayer and why God would honor our agreements.

Agreement in Man's Development

Elohim created man in His own image; He created him—male and female. Being created in the likeness of God meant Adam was given an intellect, the ability to reason; emotions, with the ability to love and demonstrate compassion; and a will, the ability to make decisions. God insured that man had everything he needed to live a productive life.

In addition, God blessed man with the spoken word: *"Be fruitful and increase in number, fill the earth and subdue it. Rule over the fish of the sea and the birds of the air and over every living creature that moves on the ground"* Genesis 1:28. There is a three-fold blessing:

1. Man was instructed to be fruitful and increase in number. Having children was meant to be a blessing for mankind.

2. Man was told to fill the earth and subdue it. The Garden had four rivers that would permit mankind to explore other territories. Mankind would have to develop mentally in order to subdue (bring into subjection) the earth. We are to learn how to use earth for the benefit of mankind.

3. Man was given the authority to rule. This responsibility would require that mankind develop in order to rule properly. It is in the position of ruler that mankind would extend the kingdom of heaven on earth.

Living out the Word of God in obedience ensures the blessing. God spoke the blessing to man; man must take His message and speak it to others. Obedience to the Word is a choice.

Adam was given freewill. God set before man the way of life and death. God did not create robots that could do only mechanical and routine tasks and commands. No, man could make choices even independent of God.

From the start man was given the responsibility to work and take care of the Garden of Eden. Assurance of man's development was generated as he handled his assignment. Because of his work, he would be able to eat freely of the trees in the Garden. Because God is sovereign, He commanded Adam not to eat of the tree of the knowledge of good and evil. As man obeyed God, God's will was done on earth as it is in heaven. Or we could say that the kingdom of God was extended to earth through man's obedience and communication with God.

It was God's purpose to establish His kingdom on earth through mankind. God's purpose for man to exercise dominion on earth has not changed. As we understand the agreements of God, we begin to realize how to move into the purpose of God and extend His kingdom on earth. We need the Word. We need to live in obedience to the Word in order to operate within the blessings spoken by God. Agreement with God ensures our development.

Agreement for Man's Redemption

Before the foundation of the world, the Godhead had agreed that Christ Jesus would be the Lamb of God to take away the sins of the world. His precious blood without blemish and without spot would be the redemption price (1 Peter 1:17 -20). God so loved the world that he freely gave His Son to die on the Cross. The Spirit of God came upon Mary for the birth of Christ (Luke 1:35). The Spirit of God was with Jesus Christ until He gave up the Spirit at death (John 19:30).

The Scriptures are clear that God does not wish that any should perish but that all would come into a saving knowledge of Jesus Christ (2 Peter 3:9). The first promise of a redeemer was given to Adam when God told him that enmity would be placed between the seed of the woman and the seed of the serpent. It is restated in another way with Abram.

God told Abram that in his seed all the families of the earth would be blessed (Genesis 12:3). The promise was passed on to David. God revealed to David that He would set up his seed after him and from his body establish his kingdom (2 Samuel 7:12-13). Jesus was identified as the Son of David.

God's redemptive program was carried forth because the agreement of the Godhead included the participation of man. As Abram obeyed God, He was declared righteous and the promise was fulfilled. David accepted that which was promised and God was able to exercise His plan.

As individuals accept God's redemption, they are moved from the power of darkness and transported into the kingdom of light. The agreements of God can be carried out as God finds individuals willing to believe and keep the conditions required. It still requires our belief and obedience for God's will to be manifested as it is in heaven. As believers we are told to go into the world and make disciples of all nations. Disciples cannot be made until individuals are taught about the Savior of the world. We as believers must realize that God does not wish that any should perish. In the obedience of mankind, God's kingdom can be extended on earth. As we make the salvation of souls our primary objective, we enter God's purposes and plans.

The first spoken Word brought light to our planet. We learn that God is light. His kingdom is called the Kingdom of Light. For believers to walk in the light and in unity with God and one another, we must know the Word of God that brings light (1 John 1:5-7) to the kingdoms of darkness.

CHAPTER FOUR

AGREEMENTS WITH MANKIND

"The Lord God formed the man from the dust of the ground, and breathed into his nostrils the breath of life; and man became a living being."
Genesis 2:7

AGREEMENTS WITH MANKIND

"Then the Lord God took the man and put him in the Garden of Eden to work it and take care of it." Genesis 2:15

The Lord God commanded the man saying, "You are free to eat from any tree in the garden; but you must not eat from the tree of the knowledge of good and evil, for when you eat of it you will surely die." Genesis 2:15-17

God gave man a command and as long as man was in agreement with God there was unity between them. God met man in the Garden, their place of communion. The agreement rested with man to maintain. Throughout history God has made agreements/covenants with mankind.

Agreement with the Word

We learn the significance of the Word from Scripture: *"All Scripture is given by inspiration of God, and is profitable for doctrine, for reproof, for correction, for instruction in righteousness, that the man of God may be complete, thoroughly equipped for every good work"* 2 Timothy 3:16-17 (NKJV).

In Genesis, Chapter 1 starting with verse 3, everything came into being by the Word. This is confirmed in the Gospel of John which states: *"In the beginning was the Word, and the Word was with God, and the Word was God. He was in the beginning with God. All things were made through Him, and without Him nothing was made that was made"* John 1:1-3 (NKJV).

The John passage alerts us that Jesus is the Word of God and the Light, which gives light to every man coming into the world (John 1:1-14). The first spoken Word brought light to the planet and it will bring light to all of us who will receive it. The Word equips us for every good work and our accomplishments needs to be done in accordance with the Word of God. The Word was significant in the creation and it is significant for us to live in agreement with God.

Agreement with Individuals

The first agreement with man was made with Adam when God placed him in the Garden with the instructions to take care of it and to leave the tree of good and evil alone.

God made an agreement with Abram concerning his Seed. He was given instruction to leave his country and family and head for an unknown country. God gave Abram promises that would be fulfilled if he obeyed God. One of the promises given Abram was that all people of the earth would be blessed through him. Abram obeyed God and his name was changed to Abraham. God fulfilled His agreement by sending His Son through Abraham and Sarah, the Seed of a woman to redeem mankind back to Him. In Christ Jesus, all people on earth can be blessed. There have been many failed agreements with mankind. Yet, God continues to stand on His agreements. For all the people on the earth to be blessed still requires individuals like us to respond to the command and go forth in the world with the gospel message. To go forth successfully requires prayers to overcome the forces of darkness, and the prayer of agreement is the key.

Jesus made an agreement with His disciples. If they would make their abode in Him and the Word, they could pray their desire and it would be done. Before Jesus left His disciples, He commanded that they go into the world and make disciples. It is up to each individual to accept or reject the agreement God has made with mankind through Christ Jesus.

The Apostle Paul understood the need of prayer in carrying out this agreement. He told the Ephesians to *"pray in the Spirit on all occasions with all kinds of prayers and requests. With this in mind, be alert and always keep on praying for all saints"* Ephesians 6:18. In addition he asked for prayer for himself: *"Pray also for me, that whenever I open my mouth, words may be given me so that I will fearlessly make known the mystery of the gospel, for which I am an ambassador in chains. Pray that I may declare it fearlessly, as I should"* Ephesians 6:18-20.

As we take advantage of God's promises and pray for Him to open the hearts of people to the Gospel, we bear fruit and become His disciples. God always intended to be in communication with man and has always given mankind the opportunity to be in agreement with Him. Are you a part of this present agreement? The last words of Jesus to His disciples were to go into the world with the good news because His blood cancels sin and restores communication with God.

The Broken Agreements

When the woman and the man ate of the tree of the knowledge of good and evil, they broke their agreement with God. Two individuals broke the agreement that disrupted fellowship with God. It also hindered God's kingdom from being established on earth as it is in heaven.

God said to Adam, *"Because you listened to your wife and ate from the tree about which I commanded you, 'You must not eat of it.' Cursed is the ground because of you... for dust you are and to dust you will return'"* Genesis 3:17-19. Death has reigned from Adam until now.

It was more than physical death that came as a result in man's broken agreement. We have seen the results of a cursed earth: droughts, volcano eruptions, floods, fires, earthquakes, and the lists goes on. God's promises can be trusted. Obedience brings blessings; disobedience brings troubles. Many things changed and unforeseen circumstances materialized when man broke his agreement with God.

The sons of Noah were instructed by God to be fruitful, multiply, and fill the earth. The blessing spoken to Adam was restored to Noah and his family. As one people, they refused to scatter abroad over the face of the earth. Instead they set out to build a city with a tower that would reach the heavens. In addition, they were out to make a name for themselves (Genesis, Chapter 11).

The Lord God came down and judged their actions. The first judgment was that nothing mankind proposed to do would be withheld from them. This we can see in our weapons of mass destruction, the chemical warfare, and even our flight to the moon. Unity can bring great accomplishments or destruction.

This answers a lot of questions as to why the Hitlers of this world are able to do much destruction. Once you understand that God has not taken back man's dominion of the earth, you will discover why it is necessary for us to request God's intervention. It is the disobedient acts of God's children that close the door to God. Our prayer of agreement opens the door between earth and heaven allowing God to respond. God honors His Word. To which of God's Words will you lay claim?

The Blood Agreement

The Godhead had agreed before the foundation of the earth that a blood sacrifice would be necessary for the atonement for the sins of mankind. The Son agreed that He would be the Lamb slain.

God shed the blood of an innocent animal to make Adam's and Eve's garments to cover their nakedness. Accepting the garments to cover themselves meant they accepted the blood sacrifice. The Hebrew word "kaphar" means, "to cover" and is also translated "atonement." Atonement brings reconciliation between God and man.

This blood sacrifice is seen again when Abel brought to God the fat portion from the firstborn of his flock. He could not have brought the fat of the animal without shedding blood. This act was an acceptance of the agreement of a blood sacrifice for a relationship with God.

After the flood when Noah came out of the ark, he *"built an altar to the Lord; and taking some of all the clean animals and clean birds, he sacrificed burnt offerings on it. The Lord smelled the pleasing aroma..."* Genesis 8:20-21. We also find Job offering blood sacrifices for his children. *"When a period of feasting had run its course, Job would send and have them purified. Early in the morning he would sacrifice a burnt offering for each of them..."* Job 1:5. Again God gave to Moses detailed instructions about the blood sacrifice. It was blood that was put on the doorpost to spare the Jews from losing their first born when the death angel passed by in Egypt. And later while in the wilderness, God charged the family of Levi with the responsibility of making sacrifices for the nation of Israel. This was to be put in place until God sent His Son, the perfect sacrifice. The daily and yearly sacrifices of the Jews demonstrated their acceptance of God's agreement to shed blood to restore their relationship with Him. As we accept Jesus Christ as Savior, we meet God's blood sacrifice and communication can be restored.

The Agreement for Restoration

God has given us Himself to restore His fellowship with mankind. Isaiah explains the work of the Godhead in bringing about salvation, the restoration of man to God.
"Yet it was the Lord's will to crush him (Jesus) and cause him to suffer, and though the Lord makes his life a guilt offering, he will see his offspring and prolong his days, and the will of the Lord will prosper in his hand" Isaiah 53:10.

Jesus took our punishment for sin. *Jesus "who, being in the form of God did not consider it robbery to be equal with God, but made Himself of no reputation, taking the form of a bondservant and coming in the likeness of men, and being found in appearance as a man, He humbled Himself and became obedient to the point of death, even the death of the cross"* Philippians 2:6-8 (NKJV).

Adam and Eve made the choice that brought loss. We can make the choice to renew our agreement with God because of the finished work of Jesus Christ on the Cross. Accepting Jesus as our blood sacrifice and covering brings restoration in our relationship with God. The agreement of restoration is done on an individual basis.

God communicated with Adam and assigned him responsibility for tending the Garden. God gave him dominion and he named each living creature. Jesus gave us, His disciples, an assignment to go into the world and make disciples; to share the message of restoration with mankind. It is our communication with God that informs us how to go and where to go.

Accepting this worldwide assignment means we will engage in spiritual warfare with the unseen forces in heavenly places. Our unseen enemy is still up to his tricks. It is crucial that we understand the magnitude of the prayer of agreement with God and one another. Maintaining an abiding relationship with Christ and the Word will open the door to communication with the Godhead that will bring answers, produce fruit, confirm our relationship as disciples, and bring glory to the Father (John 15:7-8). The Godhead has made provision for our restored agreement. It is up to us to move forward and experience open communication between heaven and earth once again. The restoration for all mankind begins as individuals accept God's provision and move forward in obedience to reach their world.

The National Agreement

God made an agreement with the nation of Israel. The blessings of this agreement is spelled out in Leviticus 26:1-12. Once you read this agreement, you wonder how the people of Israel could stray away from God. Yet, we must ask ourselves, "Are we taking advantage of our agreement with God?"

God told the nation of Israel not to make idols, images, or sacred stones because He was the Lord their God. He gave them promises that were obtainable if they followed His decrees and carefully obeyed His commands. In addition, He asked the nation of Israel to observe His Sabbath and reverence His sanctuary. These were the promises God gave them:
1. I will send rain in its season.
2. The ground will yield its crops and the trees their fruit.
3. One harvest will run into another.
4. They would eat all the food they wanted, and live in safety in the land.

5. God would grant peace in the land.
6. No one would make them afraid.
7. God would remove savage beasts from the land.
8. No sword would pass through their country.
9. They would pursue their enemies who would fall by the sword before them.
10. Five would chase a hundred and a hundred would chase ten thousand.
11. God promised to look on them with favor and make them fruitful so they would increase in number.
12. God promised to put His dwelling place among them.
13. God promised to walk among them and declared they would be His people.

From a logical standpoint, one wonders how any nation could turn their back on these precious and powerful promises. In truth, the people that first received these promises did not turn their back on them. In fact, the Scripture states: *"Israel served the Lord throughout the lifetime of Joshua and of the elders who outlived him and who had experienced everything the Lord had done for Israel"* Joshua 24:31.

The problems came over hundred years later after this whole generation died. The Scripture tell us that *"another generation grew up who knew neither the Lord nor what He had done for Israel"* Judges 3:10. Somewhere along the line, believers failed to relay God's truth to the next generation. Because they did not know God, they forsook God. This started a cycle of sin and defeat that is recorded in the Book of Judges.

Every generation needs individuals who will declare the promise of God and individuals who will fulfill the requirements of God.

The Personal Agreement

From creation, God gave man freedom to obey Him. Even today, we each must make the choice. Scripture states: *"...if anyone is in Christ, he is a new creation; the old has gone the new has come! All this is from God who reconciled us to himself through Christ and gave us the ministry of reconciliation: that God was reconciling the world to himself in Christ, not counting men's sins against them... We are therefore Christ's ambassadors, as though God were making His appeal through us"* 2 Corinthians 5:17-20a. This is a personal agreement between God and each individual accepting Christ as Savior. In Chapter 7, which covers "The Choice that Restores," we provide details on how to restore and maintain our personal relationship with God.

As God assigned responsibility to Adam, He has assigned us an important task: to be His ambassadors. This makes us diplomatic officials of the highest rank in the kingdom of God. We are to represent God, being His representatives on earth, helping to establish the kingdom of God. We can go into the world in His name and with His authority. This position is not optional. Once reconciled to God through Christ, we have this responsible position. Will you accept your ministry of reconciliation and, in obedience to Christ, go into the kingdoms of this world and make disciples?

This personal agreement is extended to the Church. This is clearly seen in Acts Chapter 13. The Church ministered to the Lord and fasted when the Holy Spirit informed the members to separate Barnabas and Saul for the mission work He had for them. The Church prayed for these servants of God, laid hands on them, and sent them forward. Would the Church be exercising more power today if they stayed focused on the mission of praying as a unit for the lost of this world?

The Prayer of Agreement

Throughout history God has had individuals that understood the need to call on Him in prayer that the people of this world would know the true God. Hezekiah understood. He prayed: *"Now, O Lord our God, deliver us from his hands, so that all the kingdoms on earth may know that you alone, O Lord, are God."* 2 Kings 19:19. The focus is to make God known with the purpose of extending God's kingdom on earth. To do this we must be in communication with God. Prayer is that communication.

In His priestly prayer, Jesus prayed that unity would be restored between God and man. Jesus said, *"That they all may be one, as You, Father, are in Me, and I in You; that they also may be one in us, that the world may believe that You sent Me"* John 17:21 (NKJV). This is the personal agreement Jesus has made with you and me. An acceptance of this agreement with Jesus means we will abide in Him and His Word as He instructed (John 15). The Lord will do what is necessary to enable us to be fruitful when we pray. This will allow each of us to co-labor with Him. We must be willing to go forward with the message. Can we afford to have the next generation being raised without knowledge of the Word; of their responsibilities; and the promises that are manifested because of their obedience? Think about this promise: *"...if two of you agree on earth about **ANYTHING** you ask for, it will be done for you by my Father in heaven"* Matthew 18:19.

I may not know your reactions to this promise, but **ANYTHING** you ask for is a mighty powerful promise for me. It appears more powerful than the promise given to the nation of Israel. What do you think?

Are you ready to accept your personal agreement?

SECTION TWO: CHOICES

CHAPTER FIVE

THE CHOICE THAT CAUSED LOSS

"...Because you have heeded the voice of your wife, and have eaten from the tree of which I commanded you, saying 'You shall not eat of it...'"
Genesis 3:17

THE CHOICE THAT CAUSED LOSS

"The Lord God took the man and put him in the Garden of Eden to work it and take care of it. And the Lord God commanded the man, 'You are free to eat from any tree in the garden, but you must not eat from the tree of the knowledge of good and evil, for when you eat of it you will surely die." Genesis 2:15-17

God's instructions to Adam were quite clear. This agreement between God and Adam ensured fellowship and kept the portal open between heaven and earth. While God freely communicated with man in the Garden, His will was being carried out on earth as it is in heaven: the kingdom of God being established on earth.

The God of eternity is always setting before us choices that can lead to life. He told his prophet Jeremiah, *"Now you shall say to this people, 'Thus says the Lord: Behold I set before you the way of life and the way of death'"* Jeremiah 21:8 (NJKV). God commanded man to eat freely from every tree with the exception of the tree of the knowledge of good and evil. God was setting before man the way of life and the way of death. He said when you eat of the forbidden tree you will surely die. It was man's choice to choose life or death.

As man took care of the Garden he would discover that the river divided into four bodies of water. Those rivers would allow him to explore other lands and discover the treasures of earth such as gold and onyx. It was God's intention to give man the opportunity to grow as he explored His creation.

Adam was given the authority to subdue the earth and have dominion over the fish of the sea, the birds of the air, and over all living things that moved on the earth. Adam exercised his authority by naming all living creatures—a demonstration of his domination over all living things. In this exercise, Adam learned that there were no helpers suitable for him. God made Adam a helper comparable to him. Adam named his wife Eve. While in obedience, man and God were in fellowship and earth and heaven were in harmony.

Interestingly, God made no mention of unseen beings to Adam. At this point, Lucifer—the anointed cherub—had fallen and was cast to the ground. He now has many names, such as serpent, Satan, devil, and dragon (Revelation 20:2). While Adam was in agreement with God, he was protected because he walked in righteousness and in his authority. The Scripture states *"in truthful speech and in the power of God; with weapons of righteousness in the right hand and in the left..."* 2 Corinthians 6:7. As Adam walked in obedience, he was protected from the unseen enemy because obedience to God is counted as righteousness. Righteousness is a weapon against our unseen enemy.

The anointed cherub was dissatisfied with his position in the heaven of heavens and exercised his freewill. He tried to exalt his throne above the stars of God and be like the most High (Isaiah 14:12-14). He wanted followers and worshipers. This broken agreement with God caused him to lose his position in the heaven of heavens. There appears to be no redemption for this fallen cherub. One third of heaven's angels followed his leadership. They, with Lucifer, were then cast to the ground. In fact, everlasting fire was prepared for him and his angels. Whenever he walked on the earth, he was under the authority of man.

He set in motion something that would change his position on the earth. His desire to be worshiped has not changed. The day arrived when the unseen enemy entered the serpent, the craftiest of all animals. His purpose was to communicate with the woman that he might deceive and entice her to eat fruit from the forbidden tree. She not only ate, but also gave to her husband Adam and he did eat. This act of disobedience broke the agreement between God and man. Man did more than lose his Garden home; he disrupted God's kingdom from being established on earth. Many unforeseen consequences were put into motion. It now requires the prayers of the righteous (James 5:16) for God's kingdom to come on earth.

We have grown accustomed to having and making choices. Too many times we fail to factor God into our choices. Choices are desirable, but the wrong choices can cause us losses. Each of us has been affected by our wrong choices. Many times it is difficult, if not impossible, to reverse the consequences of our actions. Such was the case for Adam and Eve. They made the choice that caused loss.

There are many unknown factors connected with sin. Let us turn some of our choices around. Understanding the prayer of agreement and coming into obedience with its principles will help us stop the losses. It is time to discover the hidden treasures revealed while in agreement (harmony) with God.

God's intentions have not changed for us. We have been instructed to call upon God and He has promised to answer and show us great and mighty things, which we do not know (Jeremiah 33:3). We have so many God given motivators connected with prayer.

Obedience in prayer is like being placed in the Garden of Eden with four unexplored bodies of waters. Prayer leads us in the undiscovered countries with its treasures. It is time to return to God's plan and purposes by accepting His promise to answer "**ANYTHING**" we ask in agreement with another. When we call in agreement with God and one another, the promises will be manifested. Make the choice that will reverse loss.

CHAPTER SIX

THE UNFORESEEN CONSEQUENCES

*"Don't you know that when you offer yourself
to someone to obey him as slaves,
you are slaves to the one whom you obey—
whether you are slaves to sin,
which leads to death or to obedience,
which lead to righteousness?"*
Romans 6:16

THE UNFORESEEN CONSEQUENCES

"She also gave to her husband with her, and he ate. Then the eyes of both of them were opened, and they knew that they were naked." Genesis 3:6b-7

Disobedience brought unforeseen consequences for mankind, Lucifer, and earth. Yet these acts of disobedience did not catch God unaware. Elohim knew what it would cost the Godhead by giving man freewill, the freedom to make choices. The unfolding love of God is seen in His plan of redemption. God's plan for mankind has not changed. It is still God's will that mankind be in communication with Him, just as Adam was in communication with Him in the Garden. There are wonders still to be explored as we learn to walk in agreement with God.

As it was with Lucifer, the fallen angel, so it was with Adam. There are many unforeseen consequences that accompany broken agreements with God. Adam was warned that death would be the result of breaking his agreement with God. He gave no thought to the results of his actions or to their far-reaching effects. It is not unlike the unforeseen circumstances that present themselves to us when our relationship with God is broken. We fail to get the results we want by our acts of disobedience or by our refusal to obey God.

I have wondered why God did not reveal more to Adam. Have you wondered that also? As I have pondered the thought during this study, I concluded that our obedience should come out of a love relationship for our Lord and Savior. I feel that religion has replaced our relationships with a God. Religion—faithful acts of service to God does not necessarily equate to a relationship with God.

God wants to cultivate a relationship with us. We can freely make our choices, but we have no control over the results. Let us look closely at the unforeseen consequences that faced mankind and affected the earth. In many cases, these consequences face us today. Hopefully, our study will give us understanding of what was lost and how the powerful prayer of agreement can restore our unity with God. Unity with God ensures a relationship that will bring about the will and purposes of God.

The Unforeseen Consequences with Mankind

Immediately after the act of disobedience, Adam and his wife became aware that they were naked and instinctively knew they needed a covering. This was mankind's second attempt to provide for his own needs without the help of God. God did not find their covering satisfactory. God had already put a plan into effect before the Fall and that plan included a blood sacrifice.

Before God evicted Adam and his wife from their Garden home, he killed an innocent animal and used its skin to cover them. We now know that without the shedding of blood there is no remission of sin: a factor that Adam did not know. I have sometimes wondered what type of animal gave its life. How did Adam and Eve feel when they realized an animal was killed to provide their covering? Was it an animal in which they had developed relationships? Can you image the grief they may have suffered when they had to wear these garments of skin?

In addition to losing their Garden home, Adam would now have to toil for his food. His body would return to the dust of the earth from which he had been taken. *"... for by whom a person is overcome, by him also he is brought into bondage"* 1 Peter 2:19b. That one act of disobedience gave Satan dominion over mankind and the earth. Adam had no way of knowing that his sin would affect the earth and his authority to rule.

The Unforeseen Consequences for the Earth

Man was formed from the dust of the ground, which formed some type of union. The ground was cursed for the sake of mankind. The sin of mankind and the earth has been linked in a mysterious way. Isaiah stated, *"The earth is also defiled under its inhabitants, because they have transgressed the laws, changed the ordinance, broken the everlasting covenant. Therefore the curse has devoured the earth..."* Isaiah 24:5-6b (NKJV).

The whole of earth is affected by the sin of mankind. When Jeremiah spoke to the Jews operating in disobedience, he said *"And you have defiled the land with your prostitutions and wickedness"* Jeremiah 3:2b.

Paul told the Romans that all *"creation was subjected to futility...because the creation itself also will be delivered from the bondage of corruption..."* Romans 8:20-22 (NKJV). There was no way Adam could factor this in with his act of disobedience. And there is no way for *us* to know in advance all the unknown factors that are affected by our disobedience or our unwillingness to obey.

As our unity is restored with God, we have the promise of being glorified together with Christ and, *"creation itself will also be delivered from the bondage of corruption"* Romans 8:17-21 (NKJV). This process begins as we come into agreement with God and one another, restoring the connection between heaven and earth.

The Unforeseen Consequences for Lucifer

Lucifer, the fallen angel, had walked back and forth in the midst of the fiery stones on the holy mount of God. Something Satan never considered: he would be given an enemy. God put hostility between the woman's seed and his seed.

Yes, mankind fell under his deceptive plan. Lucifer knew that if he were able to get man to obey him, man would fall under his rule, giving him dominion over mankind. At that point, he became *"the prince of the power of the air, the spirit who works in the sons of disobedience"* Ephesians 2:2 (NKJV). Man became his slave. Paul explains, *"Do you not know that to whom you present yourselves slaves to obey, you are that one's slaves whom you obey, whether of sin leading to death, or of obedience to righteousness?"* Romans 6:16 (NKJV).

Satan's deceptive plan had worked with mankind, and he endeavored to use his plan to trap Jesus, when the Holy Spirit had led Jesus into the wilderness. The devil took Jesus to an exceeding high mountain, and showed him all the kingdoms of the world and their glory, kingdoms Satan received through deception. He required Jesus to fall down and worship him. He still desires to be like the Most High and receive worship. Jesus stood on the Word; He said, *"Away with you, Satan! For it is written, 'You shall worship the Lord, your God, and Him only you shall serve'"* Matthew 4:10b (NKJV).

Satan was unable to get Jesus to obey him. That was the beginning of the unexpected. He met the Son of God, the Lamb slain before the foundation of the world—his unknown factor. Satan put in the heart of Judas Iscariot to betray Jesus, but he did not know that the Cross was God's plan for the redemption of mankind.

As Jesus was carried by the multitude to the high priest, He said to the chief priests, captains of the temple, and elders who came to Him, *"...But this is your hour, and the power of darkness"* Luke 22:52-53 (KJV). Instead of furthering his plan, Satan was instrumental in the Lamb of God going to the Cross to complete His assignment for mankind. Satan's knowledge has always been limited. God will have the last Word, for He is the Alpha and Omega, the First and the Last.

It was on the Cross that Jesus wiped out the handwriting of requirements that were against mankind and nailed them to the Cross. Jesus *"disarmed principalities and powers, He made a public spectacle of them, triumphing over them in it"* Colossians 2:15 (NKJV).

Jesus' victory on the Cross is no longer unknown, but our ability to live in that victory seems to elude us. Knowing truth and living truth requires understanding and application of that truth. In Chapter 7, "The Choice That Restores," we will look closely at how to apply God's Word for victory in our daily lives. The victory of Jesus enables us to have a relationship with God. In this relationship, the prayer of agreement is used to reverse the curse of sin and to open the portal between heaven and earth. The effects of answered prayer are not just for us, as disciples, but also for the immature believers and the unsaved. The truth must get out to everyone. The blood has been shed and the agreement between God and man is in force. Let us stop the negative unseen consequences. The promise of answered prayers and the manifestation of great and unsearchable things await the praying believers.

In all the choices that we make daily, we must make the choice that restores and maintains our relationship with Elohim. This requires a life style lived in accordance with the Word of God. Jesus has returned dominion of the earth back over to us as ambassadors and stewards. We must first ensure our commitments to be living in the victory of the sacrifice of our Savior so we are able to withstand the attack of our unseen enemy.

CHAPTER SEVEN

THE CHOICE THAT RESTORES

"How can a young man keep his way pure?
By living according to your word.
I seek you with all my heart; do not let me stray
from your commands."
Psalm 119:9-10

THE CHOICE THAT RESTORES

"Therefore, I urge you, brothers, in view of God's mercy, to offer your bodies as living sacrifices, holy and pleasing to God—this is your spiritual act of worship. Do not conform any longer to the pattern of this world, but be transformed by the renewing of your mind. Then you will be able to test and approve what God's will is—his good, pleasing and perfect will" Romans 12:1-2.

Adam was placed in the Garden of Eden with the responsibility to work and take care of it, but his dominion was the whole earth. Failing to understand the gravity of his responsibility, he ate from the forbidden tree. Interestingly, both the tree of life and the tree of the knowledge of good and evil were in the midst of the garden. I cannot help but believe that God is revealing a truth in which we must continually be aware: The choice of obedience and disobedience are always together. It is up to each of us to make the choices between obedience and disobedience—both can be attractive. One will extend the kingdom of God the other will extend the kingdoms of darkness.

Our "Garden" could be our individual homes, churches, workplaces, and/or community. As we learn to operate in these arenas, we develop our skills to reach our larger world of responsibility. Our dominion is still the world, which is why Jesus commanded His disciples to go into all nations. Our first start is to ensure our relationship with God and we can carry our kingdom of God business.

Adam had entrance to four rivers that gave him access to the rest of the earth outside the garden. Similarly, there are four areas of concern for believers who will make the choice to restore and maintain their relationship with God. I refer to these four areas as the rivers of life: personal holiness, personal humility, personal responsibility to love, and personal restraints. The choice to take advantage of our four rivers is up to each of us. When we make "the choice to restore" our relationships with God, we are then able to test and prove what God's will is for us. Acts of disobedience hinders this ability.

Obedience is God's way for us to enter into His rest and know His good pleasing, and perfect will. The Hebrew writer tells us: *"...since a promise remains of entering His rest, let us fear lest any of you seem to have come short of it. For indeed the gospel was preached to us as well as them: but the word which they hear did not profit them not being mixed with faith in those who hear it."* Hebrews 4:1-2 (NKJV). Your choice to believe demonstrates your faith, which is needed if you are to profit from His promises.

In Romans, Chapter 12, Paul urged us as believers to consider God's mercy, and offer our bodies as living sacrifices, holy and pleasing to God because this is our spiritual act of worship." We are not to be conformed to this world but transformed by renewing our mind with the Word of God. It is our individual responsibility to maintain our relationship with God. Paul tells us how to navigate these rivers that keep us in communication with God and then tells us why we should.

When you think of navigating a river, you think of the different currents. At certain times a river can provide smooth sailing. Depending on the wind and other factors, navigating the river can threaten one's life. If we are to be of value to God and His kingdom, we must learn how to navigate the rivers of life. Iniquity separates us from God and renders our prayers ineffective. Therefore, we must understand our responsibility to live in obedience to God in all areas if our prayers are to be heard. Isaiah shared this truth: *"But your iniquities have separated you from your God; your sins have hidden his face from you so that he will not hear"* Isaiah 59:2.

No one can take this journey for us. Each of us must make the decision to journey down these four rivers. It is our personal decision. Remember it is our daily choice to present our bodies as living sacrifices, which permits us to enter God's rest and know His will. The Word we read, hear and study can be profitable only if it is mixed with faith. Let us take a detailed look at how to keep our relationship with God:

Personal Holiness (vv. 1-2)

Personal holiness is a commitment to keep one's devotion to God by living in the righteousness purchased by the blood of Jesus. In a culture that puts so much emphasis on the outward body, one has to keep God's Word in focus to maintain God's standard. Paul tells us to present our body as a living sacrifice. The very term sacrifice means a willingness to give up something of value or importance for a higher cause or purpose.

Becoming intentional about avoiding those things that hinder consecration for service requires daily decisions in what we read, do, and involve ourselves. Our instructions are *to not* be conformed to this world. The only way to withstand the influence of the world is to renew our mind with the Word of God. In other words, allowing the Word to direct our thinking and actions. Worldly thinking hinders our ability to know God's will. As our minds are transformed, we are able to prove what is good and acceptable to God.

Personal Humility (vv. 3-8)

Our culture pushes confidence that borders on arrogance. We are told to stand up for ourselves and not allow anyone to take advantage of us. Paul tells believers to give some thoughts to the way we think. We are not to think more highly of ourselves than we ought. Sober thinking is the realization that God has dealt with each one of us the measure of faith. All that we have comes from God. Humility will enable us to function smoothly. We are many members in the body of Christ. Yet we have different roles or offices. Our different gifts are according to the grace that is given us.

Paul provides the following guidelines for the proper use of our gifts:
1. Prophecy–prophesy according to the portion of faith.
2. Ministry–wait on your ministry.
3. Teaching–wait on opportunity to teach.
4. Exhort–wait on opportunity for exhortation.
5. Give–do it with simplicity.
6. Ruler–rule with diligence.
7. Mercy–show mercy with cheerfulness.

Personal Responsibility to Love (vv. 9-18)

Love is the hallmark of Christianity. Our love should be sincere and without hypocrisy. Paul donates a whole chapter on love in 1 Corinthians 13. Without love, an individual is identified as being nothing and gaining nothing. Yet in this passage, Paul wants us to know how love is to operate in our lives. Again, we are provided with a practical list:

1. Abhor that which is evil and cleave to that which is good.
2. Be kindly affectionate one to another with brotherly kindness.
3. In honor, prefer one another.
4. Be not slothful in business, but fervent in spirit, serving the Lord.
5. Rejoice in hope.
6. Be patient in tribulation
7. Continue in prayer.
8. Distribute to the necessity of the saints.
9. Be given to hospitality.
10. Bless them that persecute you; bless and curse not.
11. Rejoice with them that do rejoice.
12. Weep with them that weep.
13. Be of the same mind one toward another, mind not high things, but condescend to men of low estate.
14. Be not wise in yourself.
15. Recompense to no man evil for evil.
16. Be honest in the sight of all men.
17. Live peaceably with all men.

In a world that operates contrary to God's standard, one could ask, why should we maintain actions that may open us up to abuse? The answer is quite simple: *"Because of the mercies of God"* Romans 12:1. Being created in the image of God and having been restored to the dominion of rule and authority by God's grace, we are to exercise God's grace in every circumstance.

Personal Restraints (vv. 19-21)

It takes the Spirit of God working in us to give us the proper restraints. Zerubbabel was told: *"Not by power, but by my Spirit, says the Lord Almighty"* Zechariah 4:6. Because of our fallen nature, we tend to react to situations and circumstance instead of responding by the Spirit of God.

Paul tells us how to navigate this turbulent river of self-restraint. He tells us not to avenge ourselves, but to give place unto God's wrath. He reminds us that God has total responsibility for vengeance, He will repay. Our responsibility is to love; therefore we are to feed our enemy if he or she is hungry.

We are not to allow evil to overcome us. As ambassadors for Christ, we are to overcome evil with good because it is our spiritual act of worship to a God who gave His life to us while we were yet sinners.

Jesus restored man's domination over the earth through His death on the cross. However, that relationship is only maintained in our obedience to God on a daily basis. This is our spiritual act of worship.

We must understand our responsibility to keep our lines of communication open with God while maintaining relationships with those around us. Our concern for others will motivate us to pray. Because dominion of earth has been given to mankind, God awaits our prayers that give Him the freedom to step in and respond to our needs.

Your struggles, problems, defeats, and/or concerns should be turned into prayer requests. We can enter into God's rest. This is our responsibility to invite a caring God to provide us the wisdom and insight needed and, through prayer, binds up our unseen enemies. We can only exercise our dominion while in communication with the Almighty God. Open communications ensures that His will is manifested on earth. *"Since we have these promises, dear friends, let us purify ourselves from everything that contaminates body and spirit, perfecting holiness out of reverence for God"* 2 Corinthians 7:1. Let us take up our personal responsibility.

For it is only as we live in daily victory that we can resist the temptation of our unseen enemy. Our struggles are real.

The Prayer of Agreement

God has assigned us the task of going into the world and making disciples. The devil's schemes are to keep God's kingdom from being established on earth.

As we learn what we are struggling against, we are better able to resist the enemy and to makes disciples. Until Jesus Christ returns there will be struggles. In the following chapter we will look at the tactics Satan has used and the method that will give us victory.

SECTION THREE: STRUGGLES

CHAPTER EIGHT

THE INCESSANT STRUGGLES

*"Put on the whole armor of God
so that you can take your stand against
the devil's schemes."*
Ephesians 6:11

THE INCESSANT STRUGGLES

"Finally, be strong in the Lord and in his mighty power. Put on the full armor of God so that you can take your stand against the devil's schemes. For our struggle is not against flesh and blood, but against the rulers, against the authorities, against the power of this dark world and against the spiritual forces of evil in the heavenly realms. Therefore put on the full armor of God so that when the evil comes, you may be able to stand your ground..." Ephesians 6:10-13a.

We are engaged in heavy spiritual warfare from rulers, authorities, and spiritual forces of evil in the heavenly realms that we are unable to see. Scriptures tells us that they are able to remove from the mind truth that would bring deliverance (Luke 8:12). They are sometimes able to hinder God's servants from arriving at their destination (1 Thessalonians 2:18), and are sometimes able to torment the servant of God (2 Corinthian 12:7). It becomes imperative that we navigate the rivers of life successfully so that our communications with God are open and we are not causing unbelievers to resist the gospel by our actions.

Our struggle with our unseen enemies will come to an end only when the kingdom of God is fully established on earth. This Ephesians passage alerts us to our real unseen enemies and why we need to pray in agreement with other believers so that these forces of evil can be bound. Satan and his fallen angels are still up to their schemes to defeat mankind. Yes, Jesus defeated Satan on the Cross. In God's divine plan, He has allowed Satan and his fallen angels continued access to mankind. This is why Paul has told us that our struggle is not against flesh and blood. Mankind has been in an incessant struggle against the devil and his wiles. Satan uses the fallen angels under his charge, which Paul identifies as rulers, authorities, the power of his dark world and against the spiritual forces of evil in the heavenly realms.

You may be asking yourself, "If Satan was cast out of heaven, how can these spiritual forces of evil still operate in heaven?" The Apostle Paul mentions three heavens (2 Corinthians 12:2). Satan was cast out of the third heaven, the place of God's dwelling, the heaven of heavens. The term heaven is used to speak of the sky: the space in which the sun, moon, and stars reside. This is the heaven where our enemy commands his forces. Our prayers and actions affect these forces. Jesus said, *"Whatever you bind on earth will be bound in heaven, and whatever you loose on earth will be loosed in heaven."* Matthew 18:18. We saw how this operated in the Exodus, Chapter 17. Moses and Joshua battled on both the physical and spiritual front. They bound the forces of evil empowering the forces of the Amalekites. As we understand the schemes Satan uses against us, we are better able to withstand his tactics and offer more focused prayers. As our Father responds to our prayers, the unseen realm is affected and defeated.

The Apostle John provides vital information for our victory. He states, *"Do not love the world or the things in the world...For all that is in the world—the lust of the flesh, the lust of the eyes, the pride of life—is not of the Father but is of the world"* 1 John 2:15-16 (NKJV). These worldly tools are what Satan used against Eve, against Jesus, and still uses against us. Let us look at how he used them against the woman in Genesis, Chapter 3.

Satan's Attack on the Woman

Very much aware that mankind was created in the image of God, Satan knew mankind had intelligence to reason, emotions that would allow him to enjoy the beauty around him, and a will to make decisions. Desiring to obtain rule over mankind and with it dominion of the earth, He set his scheme into effect. From his own experience, Satan knew it would only take one act of disobedience to break man's relationship with God and subjugate mankind to his rule. His need? Get mankind to disobey the one restriction God had given them. He used three worldly tools to get mankind to fall and become his slaves.

1. The lust of the flesh (attacking the will).

This unseen enemy operating through the serpent approached the woman with a question "Did God really say 'You must not eat from any tree in the Garden?'" If he was going to change the mind of this woman, he knew he must engage her in conversation.

The woman's response lets us know that the tree in the midst of the Garden (the tree of the knowledge of good and evil) should not be eaten. It brought a death sentence. Making God out to be a liar, he told the woman she would not die.

The woman saw the fruit and determined that it was good for food. She ate the forbidden fruit and gave her husband a bite. In this act, they rejected the Word of God. Satan stirred her desire to provide for her flesh. In western cultures much emphasis is placed on the flesh. Both men and women spend much time, money, and energy in losing weight, exercising the body, and even undergoing surgery to sculpt the body. More emphasis is put on outer beauty than the inward concerns for developing the fruit of the spirit.

2. The lust of the eye (attacking the emotion).

The woman saw fruit on the tree that previously she had been unwilling even to touch. As the serpent moved forward in his deceptive plan, she then saw this fruit as being pleasant to the eyes. The serpent told the woman that eating the fruit would open her eyes. Peter talked of those who walk according to the flesh, *"having eyes full of adultery and that cannot cease from sin, enticing unstable souls..."* 2 Peter 2:10-14 (NKJV).

The serpent continues to use this tool of the world to entrap unstable souls. Believers must understand how to withstand this tool of the enemy. We must navigate the rivers of life and pray. Prayers based on the Word will bind the forces that are sent to tempt us.

3. The pride of life (attacking the intellect).

The woman was told that eating this fruit would make her wise. Satan had to get the woman to change her mind about this tree of good and evil so that she would eat from it. Sometimes as I picture this scene, I see the serpent freely eating of this fruit. I think this because it says she saw the fruit was good food. It was not the fruit that would kill, it was the promise from God that eating this fruit would end with death.

This is clearly stated in Romans 6:23, *"For the wages of sin is death, but the gift of God is eternal life through Jesus Christ our Lord."* This serpent hit her on three levels, the intellect, the emotion, and her will.

These are the same tools Satan uses today to get us to reject the Word of God. As we endeavor to understand the elements of the Fall, we learn that Satan used a lie when he told the woman, "You will not surely die." He tried to discredit God by saying, *"For God knows that in the day you eat of it your eyes will be opened and you will be like God"* Genesis 3:4-5 (NKJV). They were already like God, created in His image. They had not yet developed to their full potential. He promised the woman the knowledge of good and evil and this enticed her. The rest is history.

We must ask ourselves, "How is Satan attacking us?" What hinders you from studying the Word, from praying with a partner, from sharing the gospel with an unsaved loved one? Is there a lie we need to overcome?

Satan's attack on Jesus

We learn the importance of the Word by observing how Jesus used the Word to withstand the temptations brought against Him by Satan.

1. The lust of the flesh (attacking the will).

Satan knew Jesus was hungry and suggested He turn the stones into bread. He was encouraging Jesus to use his gifts for a selfish purpose. Jesus replied, *"It is written: Man does not live on bread alone, but on every word that comes from the mouth of God"* Matthew 4:4. Jesus quoted the Word from the Book of Deuteronomy (8:3b).

Jesus knew the Word and how to use it as a defense against Satan. Obedience to the Word is a defense against the flesh. Jesus knew how to navigate the rivers of life using the Word. We must learn the Word, recover the promises in the Word, learn God's purposes for mankind, and join others in prayer in Jesus' name to live in the victory purchased for us by the shed blood of Jesus Christ.

2. The lust of the eye (attacking the emotion).

He took Jesus to a high mountain and showed Him all the kingdoms of the world and their splendor in an effort to get Jesus to bow down and worship him. Jesus responded with *"Away from me, Satan! For it is written: Worship the Lord your God, and serve Him only"* Matthew 4:10. Jesus quotes another verse from Deuteronomy (6:13).

Serve only God. Does this mean us too? One way to serve God is through prayer and fasting. This is how the prophetess Anna worshiped and served God in the temple. It states she, *"worshiped night and day fasting and praying"* (Luke 2:37). As we worship God, understand His holiness, and see His supreme greatness, our eyes will not lust for earthly things. Our focus on God is our answer against the lust of the eyes and the emotion that is attached with our desires.

3. The pride of life: (Attacking the intellect).

Satan took Jesus to the holy city and told Him to throw Himself down because the Word said the angels would lift him up. This alerts us that Satan knows how to misuse the Word. Jesus responded with, *"It is written: Do not put the Lord your God to the test"* Matthew 4:7. Jesus used another passage from Deuteronomy (6:16).

Using the Word, Jesus was submitting to God with the authority to tell Satan to get away from Him. The Apostle James tells us to submit ourselves *"to God. Resist the devil, and he will flee from you"* James 4:7. Submission to the Word and prayer are our means to obtain victory in our struggles with the unseen enemy as he tries to get us to use our intellect apart from the Word of God.

Mankind has struggled with these worldly enticements since the fall of Adam and Eve. Satan targeted their minds, their wills, and their egos (pride). This is why Paul tells the believers, *"The weapons of our warfare are not carnal but mighty in God for pulling down strongholds, casting down arguments and every high thing that exalts itself against the knowledge of God, and bringing every thought into captivity to the obedience of Christ"* 2 Corinthians 10:4-4 (NKJV).

The Word and prayer are our weapons. It takes the Word to obtain the knowledge of God so that we are able to bring every thought into captivity to the obedience of Christ. It takes the prayers of faith to accept the promise of God that brings about our victory. We do not want to test God. We want to engage Him in prayer, obtain His help and guidance to resist the enemy, and extend the kingdom of God on earth in our obedience.

CHAPTER NINE

ENGAGING THE ENEMY: UNDERSTAND HIS TACTICS

"In order that Satan might not outwit us, for we are not unaware of his schemes."
2 Corinthians 2:11

ENGAGING THE ENEMY: UNDERSTAND HIS TACTICS

"How could one man chase a thousand, or two put ten thousand to flight..." Deuteronomy 32:30.

These powerful promises in Matthew used for the purpose of God could release the will of God on earth as it is in heaven. Is this why Jesus told us to pray God's kingdom to come on earth as it is in heaven? As we begin to understand the teachings of these precepts and to meditate on these promises, we will be able to answer the question of how one man can chase a thousand and two put ten thousand to flight.

One historical account that sheds light on engaging the enemy is found in 2 Chronicles 32:1-20. The account is also recorded in Isaiah, Chapters 36 and 37. It answers some important questions: When does the enemy attack? How does the enemy attack? What can be done to resist the enemy? And how does God respond to the prayer of agreement and the actions of His people?

The 2 Chronicles and Isaiah passages reveal what is involved when you come against an overwhelming enemy. The seen and the unseen forces are working together in this historical account as Sennacherib king of Assyria sent his earthly army against Jerusalem. The prayer of agreement between King Hezekiah and the Prophet Isaiah brought marvelous results. The circumstances around this agreement allow us to gather answers for our present or upcoming battles because the evil day will come.

When Does The Enemy Attack?

King Hezekiah was a reformer in Israel. He set the house of God in order and restored temple worship. People returned to the true God and under his leadership a great number of priests consecrated themselves. He cleansed the nation and removed idols from the land. *"...He sought his God and worked wholeheartedly. And so he prospered"* 2 Chronicles 31:21b. Scripture states that after these deeds of faithfulness, *"Sennacherib king of Assyria came and invaded Judah. He laid siege against the fortified cities, thinking to conquer them for himself"* 2 Chronicles 32:1b.

We usually think that when we have obeyed God that the way becomes smooth and God is with us. After a victory, a successful ministry, or an accomplishment for the kingdom, we go our way rejoicing. The enemy desires to get us when we least expect troubles and when our guard is down. But when would you want to be attacked by the enemy? When you are walking in obedience or disobedience? After success or some type of accomplishment the enemy will try to get us to lose our faith in God. The enemy wants us to believe that our faithfulness means nothing.

How Did the Enemy Attack?

When we studied the incessant struggles with our unseen enemy, we looked at the worldly tools: the lust of the flesh, the lust of the eyes, and the pride of life. These tools are used in various ways to make us lose our faith and confidence in

The Prayer of Agreement

God, and operate in natural wisdom. Prayer should be our first response to the attack of the enemy. Look at how King Hezekiah and the Israelites were attacked:

1. *Intimidation.* King Sennacherib sent a large army and seized the fortified cities with the intent to conquer them for him. If the people made decisions by what they saw, he would weaken their spirit to fight. The reverse effect of the lust of the eyes would be in affect if King Sennacherib was able to get the Israelites to make their decision based on what they observed.

2. *Undermined the leadership.* Speaking in the language of the people, they spoke against King Hezekiah stating: *"When Hezekiah says, 'The Lord our God will save you from the hand of the king of Assyria,' he is misleading you, to let you die of hunger and thirst"* 2 Chronicles 32:10. He tried to get the Israelites to rebel against their leader by using the tool of the lust of the flesh, the fear of hunger. Their siege would keep food from coming into the cities. God works through His leaders. If the enemy can get God's people from trusting His leaders, the enemy can hinder God's plan for them.

3. *Destroy their confidence in God.* King Sennacherib challenged the ability of God to save the Israelites by using Assyria's past accomplishments in defeating the surrounding nations. They stated: *"Who of all the gods of these nations that my fathers destroyed has been able to save his people from me?"* 2 Chronicles 32:14. This was the same tactic the enemy used with Eve when he told her that *"God knows that when you eat of it (the forbidden fruit) your eyes will be open, and you will be like God, knowing good and evil"* Genesis 3:5. Satan caused Eve to doubt God's plan for her. He tried to get the Israelites to doubt God's ability to save them. This was a clear attack to get them to use their intellect. If no other nation was safe, how could they be safe?

4. *Attacked their faith: Terror.* The enemy called out in the language of the people who were on the wall *"to terrify*

them and make them afraid in order to capture the city" 2 Chronicles 32:18. Paul told the Ephesians to put on the whole armor of God; that includes the shield of faith which is able to *"extinguish all the flaming arrows of the evil one"* Ephesians 6:16. The name gives us our authority to come before God in prayer and go into the world to carry out our mission.

If the enemy had been able to terrify the Israelites, they would have been able to capture the city. The enemy attacked the faith of these people. He will attack us the same way. We need to understand the power of agreement with God and one another. *"Without faith it is impossible to please God..."* Hebrews 11:6a. *Faith is needed to stop Satan's fiery arrows and to please God.* Scripture tells us that *"some trust in chariots and some in horses, but we will trust in the name of the Lord our God"* Psalms 20:7.

5. *Provided an easy escape.* The enemy offered the people an easy way out of their problem. The men stated: *"Do not listen to Hezekiah. This is what the king of Assyria says: Make peace with me and come out to me. Then every one of you will eat from his own vine and fig tree and drink water from his how cistern, until I come and take you to a land like your own—a land of grain and new wine, a land of bread and vineyards"* Isaiah 36:16-17.

Satan gave Eve an easy path to wisdom: eat the forbidden fruit. To Jesus he offered the kingdoms of the earth without going to the cross. To the Israelites he offered them a quick solution from the siege by leaving the safety of the fortified cities to avoid hunger and thirst.

Our unseen enemy continuously operates on both the spiritual and physical plain. Singles are told they do not have to wait for marriage; they can have intimate relationships now. Students ask themselves, "Why do they have to study for an exam if I can use a cheat sheets? The list goes on. What has the enemy told you that would take you from the path of righteousness by using a shortcut? When righteousness is removed you are open to the enemy. We must make the personal commitment to holiness, humility, love, and restraint if we are to chart the rivers of life into the will and purpose of God.

We are engaged in the incessant struggle with the enemy. Will we take the path of prayer with its promised results if we have a prayer partner? Is it easier to take a few minutes and pray alone while you travel to work or do some other task? Paul told the Ephesians, *"Put on the whole armor of God so that you can take your stand against the devil's schemes"* Ephesians 6:11. He assures them the evil day will come and that they need to do what is necessary to stand (Ephesians 6:12-18). He states: *"pray in the Spirit on all occasions with all kinds of prayers and requests. With this in mind, be alert and always keep on praying for all the saints"* Ephesians 6:18.

Do you know how the enemy is attacking you, your family, your church, your community, your nation, or your world?

Are you ready for the evil day?

CHAPTER TEN

ENGAGING THE ENEMY: KNOW HOW TO RESIST

"Alarmed, Jehoshaphat resolved to inquire of the Lord, and he proclaimed a fast for all Judah. The people of Judah came together to seek help from the Lord; indeed, they came from every town in Judah to seek him."
2 Chronicles 20:3-4

ENGAGING THE ENEMY: KNOW HOW TO RESIST

"Therefore put on the full armor of God, so that when the day of evil comes, you may be able to stand your ground, and after you have done everything, to stand"
Ephesians 6:13.

Adam and Eve did not know there was an unseen being that was out to take away their authority and undermine God's plan for them. We have the benefit of their experience. We have the Word and prayer as weapons—our defense against this unseen enemy that still desires to take away our authority and undermined God's plan for our lives. Satan uses deceptive tactics to entrap mankind. There is much we can learn from studying the passages of Scriptures in 2 Chronicles Chapter 32, and Isaiah, Chapters 36-37 on how to resist the enemy. Yes, King Hezekiah found a prayer partner in Isaiah, just as Moses found one in Joshua. Moses and Joshua fought the Amalekites on two fronts, so did King Hezekiah and the prophet Isaiah fight King Sennacherib on the physical and spiritual level.

Using their pattern, we can learn how to resist the enemy. Let us examine the passages.

1. *Acknowledged the problem and prayed.* When King Hezekiah heard that the Assyrian army had come against the fortified cities of Judah, he *"tore his clothes, covered himself with sackcloth, and went into the house of the Lord"* Isaiah 37:1. This very act was one of humility and surrender to God. James told us we are to *"submit to God. Resist the devil and he will flee..."* James 4:7. Hezekiah knew how to navigate the river of humility. We see him humble himself before God and acknowledge his inability to win this war without divine help.

2. *Acknowledged His inability to win this battle.* *"...Thus says Hezekiah: 'This day is a day of trouble and rebuke and blasphemy; for the children have come to birth, but there is no strength to bring them forth.'"* Isaiah 37:3b (NKJV). Jesus said a king would not war against another king without considering whether he was able to win. Hezekiah knew they needed God's help.

3. *Acknowledged that the battle was the Lord's.* King Hezekiah knew that the enemy's true purpose was to bring reproach on the living God. He was trusting that God would hear the words of the enemy and respond. He told the people, *"Therefore lift up your prayer for the remnant that is left"* Isaiah 37:4b (NJKV). Hezekiah encouraged his people to agree in prayer. The prophet Isaiah was able to encourage the people. He told them what God said, *"Do not be afraid of what you have heard—those words with which the underlings of the King of Assyria have blasphemed me. I will have him cut down with the sword"* Isaiah 37:6-7. God indeed took this battle personally. God responded to their prayers. He has promised to answer our prayers of agreement. The river of restraint is being navigated here, as they believe God to avenge them.

4. *Consulted with the military officials.* King Hezekiah talked with his military officials. *"When Hezekiah saw that Sennacherib had come and that he intended to make*

war on Jerusalem, he consulted with his officials and military staff..." 2 Chronicles 32:2 (NKJV). Scripture states that, *"wisdom is found in those who take advice"* Proverbs 13:10b. King Hezekiah met with his officials and military staff. As they agreed on what action should be taken against the enemy, they were placing themselves where God would command a blessing.

As we come together in the prayer of agreement, we should take time to discuss the issues, obtain advice from one another, and seek God's help together.

5. *Blocked the enemy from utilizing their resources.* They determined to *"block all the springs and the stream that flowed through the land"* 2 Chronicles 32:3 (NKJV). This important step in resisting the enemy was to keep them from using their resources. This is a truth we must learn. One of our resources is finances. Satan uses the lust of the eye. Many believers are in financial debt and do not pay their tithes. This opens them up to the devourer, Satan (Malachi 3:10-11).

Another major resource is our children. They need to be taught how to love the Lord and resist the tactic of the devil, a responsibility given to parents (Deuteronomy 6:4-7). Instead, many Christian parents are buying their children books and videos like Harry Potter, which exposes them to the occult. We are losing too many of our children to this world. It is time we develop plans to keep the enemy from using our children

6. *Repaired the broken walls.* *"Then he worked hard repairing all the broken sections of the wall and building towers on it. He built another wall outside that one and reinforced the supporting terrace of the City of David"* 2 Chronicles 32:5a. It sometimes takes an attack from the enemy to reveal the cracks in our defense. What have you discovered is open to the enemy? How are you repairing the broken walls that leave your family and church exposed to Satan's entry?

7. *Made weapons.* "*He also made large numbers of weapons and shields*" 2 Chronicles 32:5b. If one is going to win in a war, there must be weapons with which to fight. They took the time to identify and make their weapons. Here they are navigating the river of holiness the greatest weapon of all. Righteousness is a weapon (2 Corinthian 6:7). We are told our weapons are not carnal. Look at what you are fighting with. Are you and a prayer partner using the power of agreement by praying the Word?

8. *Military officers were appointed.* King Hezekiah knew if there were to be any victory, the people would need leadership and encouragement. "*He appointed military officers over the people and assembled them before him in the square at the city gate...*" 2 Chronicles 32:6. Jesus knew we would need leadership and gave to the church apostles, prophets, evangelists, and some pastors and teachers (Ephesians 4:11). Paul tells us to fight a good fight. Have we included prayer partners to help us in our spiritual battles against the kingdom of darkness? Do we follow the guidance of our spiritual leaders?

9. *Encouraged the people.* It would be hard to win a battle with discouraged people. King Hezekiah encouraged his military officers and the people with these words, "*Be strong and courageous. Do not be afraid or discouraged because of the king of Assyria and the vast army with him, for there is a greater power with us than with him*" 2 Chronicles 32:7. Hezekiah was aware of the unseen forces that were at work in their behalf. Are we?

The power of agreement in prayer can be a major source of encouragement to the believers who learn that God honors His promises. He watches over His Word to perform it (Jeremiah 1:12). Isaiah told us that God's Word would not return to God empty. His Word will accomplish what He pleases and it will prosper in the things for which God sent it (Isaiah 55:11). This places you and me in partnership with

God. We pray His Word and extend His kingdom on earth. What more encouragement would we need?

10. *Acknowledged the presence of the Lord.* The people were told that God with them was a greater power than the enemy and that God would fight the battle. With Sennacherib *"is only the arm of flesh, but with us is the Lord our God to help us and to fight our battles. And the people gained confidence from what Hezekiah the king of Judah said"* 2 Chronicles 32:8. King Hezekiah knew that this battle was more than the army of flesh. He knew to engage the help of God, which allowed them to get help from heaven.

11. *Did not engage the enemy in conversation.* The king instructed the people not to respond to the enemy. *"But they held their peace and answered him not a word; for the king's commandment was, 'Do not answer him'"* Isaiah *36:21* (NKJV). The fall of mankind began with Eve's discussion with the serpent. We cannot win talking with a deceptive enemy.

12. *The prayer of agreement.* *"King Hezekiah and the prophet Isaiah son of Amoz cried out in prayer to heaven about this. And the Lord sent an angel, who annihilated all the fighting men and the leaders and officers in the camp of the Assyrian king"* 2 Chronicles 32:20-21a.

God desires to co-labor with His children. Hezekiah and Isaiah met God's requirement as they cried out to Him in prayer. Their prayer and their actions of trust in God enabled God to annihilate all the fighting men of the Assyrian army. Heaven and earth were connected and an angel from heaven annihilated the fighting men on earth. God's promise was fulfilled.

Understanding the tactics of the enemy and the methods used for victory will enable us to restore what has been lost in this fallen world. Because Jesus told his disciples to pray for God's kingdom to come and His will to be done on earth as it is in heaven, we must believe that prayer is the key for the kingdom to be extended on earth. Will you use this truth you hold?

Would you like His kingdom established in your situation? If this is your desire, you must evaluate the situation and determine what actions are needed to accompany your prayers. In other words, what has God's word said about the situation? Do you know someone who will help you carry this burden in prayer?

How can one chase a thousand and two put ten thousand to flight? Samson single handedly killed one thousand men with a jawbone because the Spirit of the Lord came mightily upon him (Judges 14:14-15). You and your praying partner will experience the work of the Holy Spirit. With the prayer of agreement between King Hezekiah and the Prophet Isaiah, over one hundred and eighty-five thousand men in the Assyrian army were put to death by an angel of the Lord (Isaiah 37:36). Two men in prayer experienced God's deliverance of over 85,000 of their enemies. The miraculous can happen. It can happen on *your* behalf.

SECTION FOUR: REPOSITIONING

CHAPTER ELEVEN

REPOSITIONING OURSELVES WITH GOD

*"I looked for a man among them who
would build up the wall and
stand before me in the gap on behalf of the land
so I would not have to destroy it, but I found none."*
Ezekiel 22:30

REPOSITIONING OURSELVES WITH GOD

"He stood between the living and the dead and the plaque stopped." Numbers 16:48

As we have discussed, the fall of mankind brought about many unforeseen consequences. There was a shift in the power structure, man lost his dominion over the earth, mankind became a slave to Satan, and everyone born into the world is born a sinner. Through the history of mankind, God has searched for that one person who would understand. *"Go up and down the streets of Jerusalem, look around and consider, search through her squares, if you can find but one person who deals honestly and seeks the truth, and I will forgive the city"* Jeremiah 5:1.

God continues on the lookout for that individual or individuals who seeks truth and deals honestly. In other words, He is seeking for individuals who have made the personal decision to navigate the rivers of live. The journey begins with holiness, which is obtained as we are transformed by the Word and accept our new life in Christ. It flows out into personal humility, as we understand that all we have has come from God and our gifts are to be used to profit all mankind. One cannot navigate far in this life without the love of God being shed apart abroad in our hearts by means of the Holy Spirit. And because we still operate in a fallen world, there must be personal restraints so that we will not be overcome with evil. With prayer and the word of God, we are able to navigate through these rough waters.

For the sake of the righteous, God will forgive the city. As we reposition ourselves with God, our lives will reflect His love and allow His grace, rather than wrath, to be poured out on the unbelievers. God is in search of those who understand the truth that their lives are to hold back judgment until the Kingdom of God is established on earth.

The prayer of agreement and the commitment of individuals who share God's heart for mankind are necessary if we are to reposition ourselves with God. God desires a relationship with all mankind.

A relationship of purpose and significance awaits us as we move in obedience. Jesus told His disciples that all authority in heaven and on earth was given to Him. Before His death and resurrection, Jesus gave His disciples the authority to use His name (John 14:13-14). In His name we go and make disciples of all nations.

We have the message that communication between God and man can be restored to mankind in Christ Jesus. Because the enemy of mankind is still active, believers need to exercise their authority for these unseen enemies to be bound and for captive mankind to be released.

As you and I move into the purpose and plans of God, we reposition ourselves with Him to accomplish His purpose. God's Word reveals truth. When God told Adam that he would die if he ate from the forbidden tree, Adam ate, died and his body returned to dust.

The first death was separation from God by sin, which caused all mankind to be born in this separation. Yet, Adam did not immediately drop dead physically. According to

Scripture Adam lived on earth for nine hundred and thirty years before experiencing physical death. God was patient.

Peter informed us that God is patient. *"The Lord is not slow to keeping his promise, as some understand slowness. He is patient with you, not wanting anyone to perish, but everyone to come to repentance."* 2 Peter 3:9. Repositioning ourselves with God is understanding why He exercises patience with us. He wants us to exercise our dominion on earth by standing in the gap before Him on behalf of those who are perishing.

Do not underestimate your importance in the plans and purposes of God. One person can make a difference. As we understand God's love for all mankind and understand the importance of prayer, we can help implement the promises God has given to all mankind. We stand in the place of life and death.

God's plan for mankind has not changed. The blood of Jesus has been shed for the sins of all mankind. This is our gospel message. God does not desire that any should perish, so we who know the Lord must stand in the gap using the prayer of agreement to reposition ourselves with God. Once in communication with God, we can speak God's Word and His promises back to Him. Then a rebellious people can be spared.

Moses and Aaron stood in agreement in their desire to hold back the wrath of God from this newly formed nation. In rebellion, the Israelites rejected Moses and Aaron as their leader. God brought judgment with a plague. The love of Moses and Aaron for the people caused them to reposition themselves. They stood in the gap between God and the people under judgment.

Moses and Aaron in agreement fell on their faces before God. Moses directed Aaron to take a censer with fire and incense and make atonement for the people. That day 14,700 people died in the plaque. More would have died if Moses and Aaron had not come together with their prayer request. Aaron quickly ran and stood between the living and the dead, stopping the plague (Numbers 16). God is looking for us to stand on His Word and stop the judgments. God keeps His promises, *"For all the promises of God in Him are Yes, and in Him Amen, to the glory of God through us" as we accept these promises* 2 Corinthians 1:20 (NKJV).

God's Word is given for us to live by. The prophet Isaiah tells us of God's promise to honor His Word, *"So shall My word be that goes forth from My mouth; It shall not return to Me void, but it shall accomplish what I please and it shall prosper in the things for which I sent it"* Isaiah 55:11(NKJV). The key to God's promises is to believe them, tell God you accept them, and return the Word to God in prayer.

SECTION FIVE: PRAYER

CHAPTER TWELVE

THE HEART OF GOD

*"I urge, then, first of all, that requests, prayers, intercession
and thanksgiving be made for everyone—
for kings and all those in authority,
that we may live peaceful and quiet lives
in all godliness and holiness.
This is good, and pleases God our Savior,
who wants all men to be saved..."*
1 Timothy 2:1-4a

THE HEART OF GOD

"I have other sheep that are not of this sheep pen. I must bring them also. They too will hear my voice, and there shall be one flock and one shepherd." John 10:16

Jesus Christ identified Himself as being the Good Shepherd, one that would lay down His life for the sheep (John 10:11). His sheep included not only the nation of Israel, but *all* who would hear His voice and come out of the world into His flock. And indeed, He laid down His life for mankind. The God of peace brought Jesus back from the dead as the Great Shepherd of the sheep. Now the blood of the everlasting covenant makes us perfect in every good work to do His will. He works in us that which is well pleasing in His sight through Jesus Christ (Hebrews 13:20-21).

The amazing thing about the heart of God is that He has included us, His disciples, into His plan. We are to be His voice and go into the world and make disciples from every nation. The love of God should be our motivating factor to go into the world with His love story that would include all mankind.

The entire Bible reveals the heart of God for the lost and rebellious. One passage that touches my heart is found in Ezekiel, Chapter 22. The Israelites had shed much innocent blood. The Lord asked His prophet Ezekiel to judge the blood city and show her all her abominations.

Every level of society was unfaithful. God identified her sins. Her priests, who had the responsibility to teach the people and lead them in worship, were themselves violating the law. The priests made no distinction between the holy and unholy or the clean and unclean. They had no respect for the Sabbath and profaned God among themselves. What chance did the people have when those that should be teaching them were going astray?

God said the princes, her civic leaders, were like wolves. They were destroying the people for dishonest gain. If that was not enough, the prophets who were God's spokesmen were not on the job either. They were giving the people false visions and divining lies. When God had not spoken, they were giving the people messages that were not from God. With no godly guidance from the priest, the princes or the prophets, the people of the land were left to their own devices. They oppressed the people, committed robbery, and mistreated the poor and needy. They were no better to the stranger that they oppressed. They were instructed not to vex a stranger, nor oppress him, because they were once strangers in Egypt (Exodus 22:21). The whole nation was far from God and His standard.

God saw all the evil, yet it was not in His heart to destroy. God sought for a righteous man among them, who would stand in the gap between himself and these sinners that where headed for judgment. The prayer of the righteous can make up a wall to hold back God's judgment. God could not find one person who would stand in the gap before Him and the land, so he had to pour out His judgment. Would God find you standing in the gap?

Another example of God reaching out to the lost is seen in the book of Jonah. God was sending His best to an evil people who did not know Him. Jonah was a statesman as well

The Prayer of Agreement

as a prophet. He served during the reign of King Jeroboam II in the northern kingdom. Jonah was a native of Gath-hepher (2 Kings 14:25).

The Lord used Jonah to provide King Jeroboam with information that allowed him to restore the boundaries of Israel. King Jeroboam reigned for 41 years and was judged evil. Yet God responded to the suffering of his people because there was no one to help them. Because Jonah served his people, he willingly proclaimed God's Word to the evil king.

However, the day came when God called Jonah to go to Nineveh—a wicked and evil city that was an enemy to Israel. Nineveh was the capital of the Assyrian Empire, which dominated the ancient near East for about three hundred years. This ancient city rose to power about the time of the divided Hebrew Kingdom. Over time, it had absorbed and destroyed the northern kingdom of Israel. This was one of the first of the kingdoms of man. Nimrod, a mighty hunter, built it.

Jonah, knowing the heart of God, did not want this mission assignment and went off in the opposite direction to Tarshish. Jonah knew God was gracious to the Northern Kingdom of Israel, but did not want to see God's grace shown to the wicked city of Nineveh, his enemy. God did not let Jonah off the hook, but instead began to show His prophet that it was not profitable to reject God's assignment.

Hopping a ship to Tarshish from the presence of the Lord, his flight was interrupted by a mighty tempest in the sea. His disobedient act put other lives in danger and caused those on the ship to lose their cargo. Thrown overboard to save the lives of the sailors and the ship, Jonah landed in the belly of a fish for three days and three nights.

Out of affliction, Jonah prayed to the Lord his God and agreed to pay his vows. The Lord spoke to the fish and it vomited Jonah upon dry land. This time Jonah responded in obedience when God said. *"Arise, go unto Nineveh"* Jonah 3:1 (KJV).

He preached with such power that the people believed God. They proclaimed a fast and put on sackcloth, from the greatest of them to the least of them. Even the king of Nineveh arose from his throne, took off his robe, covered himself with sackcloth and sat in ashes. They even put the beasts, herds, and flocks on a fast, keeping food and water from the animals.

It took Jonah three days to journey through the city preaching, *"forty days and Nineveh shall be overthrown"* Jonah 3:4b. When God saw the response of the people He repented of the evil intended for them.

Our natural reaction is to rejoice whenever we have a positive response to our ministry. However, this was not the case with Jonah. Jonah was a *prophet* of God without *the heart* of God. God is patient, *"not wanting anyone to perish, but everyone to come to repentance"* 2 Peter 3:9b. When God's word was preached and the nation repented, God's purpose for sending Jonah to Nineveh was graciously accomplished.

The heart of God was even manifested in the way he dealt with His rebellious prophet. Jonah just wanted to die when he realized Nineveh was not going to be destroyed. He actually gives God the reason for not wanting to preach in Nineveh. Jonah told God, *"for I knew that you are a gracious and compassionate God, slow to anger and abounding in love, a God who relents from sending calamity"* Jonah 4:2.

God dealt graciously with Jonah. He told Jonah, *"Nineveh has more than a hundred and twenty thousand people who cannot tell their right hand from their left, and many cattle as well. Should I not be concerned about that great city?"* Jonah 4:11.

Are you aware of the heart of God? And if you are, how willing are you to offer prayers with a partner to stand in the gap for that family, that church, that community, and /or that nation in opposition to God. God is looking for that one to stand in the gap before Him so He can withhold judgment and not destroy (Ezekiel 22:30). As long as there are evil and rebellious people in this world, you and I are on assignment.

In God's search, will He find you?

CHAPTER THIRTEEN

THE HEART OF GOD'S INTERCESSOR

*"But Moses and Aaron fell face down and cried out,
O God, God of the spirits of all mankind, will you be angry
with the entire assembly when only one man sins?"*
Numbers 16:22

THE HEART OF GOD'S INTERCESSOR

"...far be it from me that I should sin against the Lord in ceasing to pray for you..." 1 Samuel 12:23b (NJKV).

Samuel, the last judge of Israel and God's prophet, understood his role as a servant of God. Even when he was carrying out his responsibility to declare the great wickedness of Israel to demand a king, Samuel knew how to stand before God in their behalf. They had rejected God from being their King. Having the heart of an intercessor, he told the Israelites that he would not sin against the Lord by ceasing to pray for them. Most of us have never thought it sinful not to pray on behalf of others.

It was Paul, an apostle of Jesus Christ, that exhorted believers that first and foremost *"that supplication, prayers, intercessions, and giving of thanks be made for all men, for kings and all who are in authority, that we may lead a quiet and peaceable life in all godliness and honesty. For this is good and acceptable in the sight of God our Savior"* 1 Timothy 2:1-3 *(NKJV).*

God calls for all believers to pray. He desires His kingdom to be established on earth. When we develop the heart of an intercessor, we will have a heart like God. In prayer we can

The Prayer of Agreement

learn to stand between the living and the dead and intercede for life. God responded to the prayers of Moses and Aaron who stood in the gap for the children of Israel and held back God's judgment.

As we take a close look at how Moses and Aaron stood in the gap, we can learn much about the heart of an intercessor. Our account is recorded in Numbers, Chapter 16. It opens with Korah, a son of Levi, and Dathan and Abiram, sons of Reuben, coming before Moses to oppose His leadership. They brought with them two hundred and fifty princes of the assembly, famous in the congregation and men of renown.

Reading the account of this rebellion, I could see the deceptiveness of the flesh. It is from the tribe of Levi that God called out Aaron and his sons to serve as His priest. Korah was from the tribe of Levi, but was not a descendent of Aaron so did not qualify to be a priest. Reuben was the eldest son of Israel, but because he defiled his father's bed, he lost his birthright as the elder son. Korah, Dathan and Abiram gathered against Moses and Aaron to reject their leadership and to declare themselves and the congregation holy because the Lord was among them. They had the backup support of the famous men of renown, but not the support from the Word of God.

The flesh did not approve of God's leadership as they thought more highly of themselves then they ought. They had no idea of what holy is and what holiness does. Both Moses and Aaron realized immediately that these men were placing themselves in danger of destruction. Moses fell upon his face before God. In addition he tried to talk some sense into them.

He told Korah and his company that the Lord would show who is holy and who are His, and would cause His chosen to come near unto him. Moses sent for Dathan and Abiram, but they would not come. Instead they charged Moses with making himself a prince over them. Korah (one of the leaders

The Prayer of Agreement

of the Levi tribe) gathered the congregation against Moses and Aaron at the entrance of the Tent of Meeting.

When God told Moses and Aaron to separate from among the congregation, that He could destroy them, they fell upon their face and prayed to God. They asked God not to be angry with the entire congregation. Moses continued to do what was necessary to keep the children of Israel from being destroyed by God. Moses rose up and went to both Dathan and Abiram.

Moses told the congregation to depart from these wicked men. The assembly moved away from the tents of Korah, Dathan, and Abiram. Because they obeyed Moses, their lives were spared. God caused the ground to open up and they were swallowed up with their houses and everything they owned. The earth closed over them.

There are several things we learn about the heart of an intercessor from this chapter.

1. *Must have the heart of God.* Moses knew that even in God's wrath, He desires to deliver. One must know that God looks for the intercessor. A Jeremiah passage reveals this truth: *"Go up and down the streets of Jerusalem, look around and consider, search through her squares. If you can find but one person who deals honestly and seeks the truth I will forgive the city."* Jeremiah 5:1. If you were that only believer, would God find you praying for the lost?

2. *Must be aware the actions that will bring judgment from God.* Moses was willing to intercede on behalf of those in danger. When Kohath, the Levi, Dathan and Abiram the sons of Reuben challenged the authority of Moses and Aaron, the first act of Moses and Aaron was to fall upon their face before God. They knew that these men were doing more then challenging them. They were challenging God and the authority He put in place.

3. *Must have a heart of compassion for those that are coming against you.* You must remember that the unseen

enemy motivates the rebellious. If you respond wrongly to the attacks against you, Satan has gotten you and those that come against you. Moses tried talking with Kohath. He wanted him to understand that God had already separated the Levites to be near Him and do service in the tabernacle. Moses reveals their real motive for their rebellion. Because of the pride of life, they wanted the priesthood also.

4. *Must operate in humility.* When Moses contacted Dathan and Abiram to talk with them, they refused to come to him. Moses however went to them. They refused to submit to Moses' leadership. In humility, Moses went to them.

5. *Must be willing to stand in the gap and intercede for the people.* God told Moses and Aaron to separate from the congregation and He would put an end to them. Moses and Aaron, in agreement to spare the lives of this rebellious crew, fall on their faces before God. Korah was evidently the leader of this group and Moses interceded with God not to judge the congregation by one man's sin. Instead of the whole assembly being destroyed, only those who refused to submit were destroyed.

6. *Must be unselfish.* Moses and Aaron were completely unselfish. They did not try to defend themselves. They lifted the problem up to God. God confirmed His chosen leaders by opening the earth and swallowing up the rebellious. In addition fire came from the Lord and consumed the two hundred and fifty men that offered incense. These men were identified as men of renown, but only in the eyes of the people. They were not viewed as such in God's eyes. They were rebels.

7. *Must understand that promotion comes from God.* It is normal for individuals to look at those in leadership and desire that position. There is, however, a big difference in desiring a position of leadership and trying to overthrow it. Yet to be in God's place of leadership can put you in a position of envy. Navigating the river of life becomes even more

crucial because you must still stand in the gap for those that want your position or are trying to unseat you.

Because of the faithfulness of Moses and Aaron who stood together in the power of agreement, the congregation of Israel was spared. Can God count on you? Would you have a heart to intercede for those who are after your position? This is certainly not an easy situation, but it would take the heart of God to respond rightly. Once we know what is at stake, we should be willing to stand in the gap.

The blessings given to Adam and Noah are still in effect. We are the family of Noah and so is every family on the face of the earth. Jesus said He came that we might have life and have it more abundantly. I believe that still means we are to be fruitful, increase in number, and subdue the earth. The only way we are able to rule well is to remember that we are Ambassadors of Christ. We have the responsibility to pray in the name of Jesus as we navigate the rivers of life that will take us into the world. Our prayers and actions on earth will influence what is happening in the heavenly realm. When our agreements bring forth answers from God, we will see more and more individuals coming into the kingdom of God being translated from the kingdom of darkness into the kingdom of light.

No, our struggles will not stop until our Savior returns. But in the meantime we can stand in the gap, engage the enemy, and with our prayer partner reposition ourselves with God and exercise the dominion that was returned to us by Christ Jesus. God desires a relationship with all mankind, and we believers must play an essential role for God's plan to become a reality.

As we gather in the name of Jesus, let us influence what happens in the heavenly realm with the prayers of agreement giving our Father in heaven His Word and promises to act upon.

Today is a good time to cash in that promissory note.

CPSIA information can be obtained at www.ICGtesting.com
Printed in the USA
BVOW041341070413

317454BV00001B/24/P